INVOKING THE WILD SOUL OF MUSIC

"As a child, piano virtuoso Hélène Grimaud heard her first concerts in the sounds of Nature. It was here, in Nature, that music came alive and her life's path was forged. Her memoir, *Invoking the Wild Soul of Music*, is a testament to the profound impact Nature can have on one's life, starting with passion, leading to profession, and ultimately finding purpose."

PAM MONTGOMERY, AUTHOR OF
PLANT SPIRIT HEALING AND
CO-CREATING WITH NATURE

INVOKING THE WILD SOUL OF MUSIC

HÉLÈNE GRIMAUD

with Stéphane Barsacq

Translated by Jon E. Graham

Inner Traditions
Rochester, Vermont

Inner Traditions
One Park Street
Rochester, Vermont 05767
www.InnerTraditions.com

Originally published in French in 2023 under the title *Renaître* by Éditions Albin Michel
First U.S. edition published in 2026 by Inner Traditions

Cataloging-in-Publication Data for this title is available from the Library of Congress

ISBN 979-8-88850-215-0 (print)
ISBN 979-8-88850-216-7 (ebook)

Printed and bound in India at Replika Press Pvt. Ltd.

10 9 8 7 6 5 4 3 2 1

Text design and layout by Priscilla Harris Baker
This book was typeset in Garamond, with Brother 1816 and Gill Sans used as display typefaces

To send correspondence to the author of this book, mail a first-class letter to the author c/o Inner Traditions, One Park Street, Rochester, VT 05767, and we will forward the communication.

CONTENTS

	Foreword by Stéphane Barsacq	vii
	Overture	xv
1	The Oceanic Sense of Life	1
2	Between Europe and the United States	21
3	Initiations	41
4	Music Will Save the World	57
5	At the Piano	77
6	The Rebel Soul	98
7	Approaches to Romanticism	114
8	Intimacies	128
9	More on Love	142
10	Ecofeminism	159
11	Spiritual Motherhood	175
12	Horse Whisperer	188
	Coda	201
Appendix	A Short Portable Philosophy	203

What to do, you may ask, in times of horror and turmoil? Exactly. In the midst of this darkness, it's necessary to see things clearly.

André Suarès

FOREWORD

Stéphane Barsacq

Hélène Grimaud and I discussed this book many times. The first time was in New York one memorable spring, when I went to the Wolf Center* and Hélène allowed me to get close to the wolves—at a safe distance, I might add. What I saw stunned me in the strongest sense: she was at one with these wild animals, just as she had been earlier with the works of Brahms. There was no hesitation; on the contrary: wild and graceful, the intimate unfolding of the whole being. Years have passed, Hélène Grimaud has not stopped performing on five continents, and she has remained at the forefront of conservation, writing books and giving interviews. The project I proposed became all the more necessary, but also all the more delicate. We didn't want a book that would repeat her three previous books, which form a trilogy that begins in Aix-en-Provence, her birthplace, and continues in Paris, where she was educated, and ends when she went to the United States—as described in *Wild Harmonies. Leçons particulières*†—follows her paths through Italy and Germany, and at the end of this long

*The Wolf Conservation Center.

†Private Lessons.

journey she comes back to her beloved wolves in *Retour à Salem.** In the same spirit, we wanted a book that was new and that would allow us to do what even the best newspaper interview can't do, no matter where it is or how big it is—which is to connect with time. In fact, this book was constructed month by month, with a lot of back and forth that forced us to better define the questions and answers. I remember talking about it with the writer Yves Bonnefoy, who shared with me his conviction that writing must be the opposite of filling pages; for him, he said, "writing hardly begins until it is rewritten, because then a *self-awareness* can emerge, a movement in which we understand ourselves, or better still, in which we can *understand ourselves again.*"

On the threshold of this book, I'd like to say a few brief words about Hélène Grimaud, seen from near and far in the course of her transformation and the work that has made her cherished by music lovers the world over, but also to young people in love with nature, and to those who know how wholehearted she is in her choices, and that nothing she undertakes is trivial. She achieves nothing by any other means than what brings energy and clarity, passion and hope, to everyone. By chance, we've known each other for a long time and have often been brought together for tours or books like *Le Piano dans l'éducation des jeunes filles,*† my novel, which I read to her chapter by chapter. If there's one thing that strikes me about Hélène Grimaud, it's her liveliness, which never sleeps. Everything interests her. She knows that everything can enrich her relationship with music, but it's no less striking that this artist works nonstop with a dis-

---

*Return to Salem.

†Piano in the Education of Young Girls.

cipline that compels admiration—she never takes anything for granted. She hardly ever looks to the past. Her goal is to become better and better in all areas, based on an uplifting view of the meaning of life. Thus she is always young, and those who come close to her feel rejuvenated by her invigorating contact, as if she had been able to see the source where what matters are not the latest novelties, but, on the contrary, the reference points where the origin of what will never end can be found.

Hélène Grimaud has already achieved a great deal, although it seems only yesterday that she was unanimously awarded first prize at the Paris Conservatory at the age of thirteen. On the musical level, she conquered the heights of classical music with records that have become benchmarks; from Bach to Chopin, from Mozart to Liszt, from Debussy to Bartók or Shostakovich, not to mention her doubles, Beethoven, Schumann, and Brahms, composers whom she has been able to bring to life with contemporary musicians such as former subjects of the USSR like the Estonian Arvo Pärt or the Ukrainian Valentin Silvestrov, but also the American John Corigliano or the Japanese Tōru Takemitsu. Whether playing as a soloist, as part of a duo, or with an orchestra, she knows how to bring out every nuance. She even recorded Brahms's *Lullaby* at the request of our friend Françoise Hardy who sang the lyrics. And who knows, maybe one day her plan—she loved Jean Ferrat and he loved her—to sing a duet with Sting will come true? From disc to disc, Hélène Grimaud has demonstrated an imagination that can't help but recall the dresses from Perrault's fairy tale: the moon-colored dress, the sun-colored dress, and the sky-colored dress.*

*From "Donkeyskin" by Charles Perrault.

Over the years, the paradoxes inspired by this artist have not gone unnoticed. Who is this young woman whose charisma has captured me, as it has all those who have met her, and who is able to deal with wild animals on a familiar basis? Who is this both simple and refined pianist who is able to sing together with the most feared of all animals? Who is this concert artist accustomed to great halls who lived in the wilderness on the heights above Salem? Of course there are those who have pointed out the similarities between Hélène Grimaud and wolves. Don't they share the fact of being rebellious, nomadic, exiled, untouchably strong, and a scapegoat for those who feel weakened by what outshines them? The poet Philippe Jaccottet speaks of "high signs" when speaking of her, and the painter Balthus and the filmmaker Ingmar Bergman, some of the greatest artists, could see what she brought to the table: in a separate, closed, smothered, and smothering world, Hélène Grimaud seemed not only to be a musician, but also to be musical, to claim with all her being the union of being and world, intimately united. Undoubtedly, this union, which exalts our nostalgia and guides our desire, is an illusion. But that's the nature of music when it comes to embodiment, to what Fauré's friend Charles Van Lerberghe once called "glimpses." In this way, with Hélène Grimaud, we are *here and elsewhere,* and she herself always seems, at the moment when she is most present, to be on the verge of disappearing into the unknown, leaving us dissatisfied and longing for reunion, like a score known by heart that anticipates our memory by offering the consecration of a future in which everything becomes possible and free again.

I must say a few words about what I consider to be one of Hélène Grimaud's strengths. I am speaking about her commitments.

With the clearest humanist awareness she knew from the beginning that it was necessary to match her words with her deeds. So, despite her critics, she has taken risks to fight on a practical level for the preservation of nature, be it the environment, endangered species, or even, more recently, horses, which some would prefer to slaughter. Likewise, how can we fail to admire her desire to emphasize feminine qualities, as other great female musicians in the past have done, from Maria Yudina to Martha Argerich, and in the process to destroy macho prejudices about female musicians, who are in no way inferior to male musicians in terms of conception, virtuosity, or poetic imagination? Aware of her differences, Hélène Grimaud has shown how to turn them into strengths. With the same fervor, she has embraced the highest musical tradition, fought for a better world, and treated Mozart or Brahms with the same love as wolves, which she considers to be essential to our future as works of art. If by chance all wild species were to be exterminated, we would soon follow! Steeped in German Romanticism, running from Novalis* to Hölderlin† and including musicians, painters, philosophers, and scientists alike, but also steeped in the world of the Native Americans where she loves to spend time, always searching for the union of opposites that enriches the whole, Hélène Grimaud is an artistic and political example of a person who understands the ultimate meaning of freedom: the ability to say NO in the name of a higher purpose.

Over the years, we have seen her play as a soloist or with such

*The pen name of Georg Philipp Friedrich Freiherr von Hardenberg (1772–1801), German aristocrat, poet, novelist, philosopher, and mystic.

†Johann Christian Friedrich Hölderlin (1770–1843) was a German poet and philosopher and a key figure of German Romanticism.

remarkable artists like Truls Mørk, Jan Vogler, or Sol Gabetta, as well as Renaud Capuçon, Rolando Villazón, or Thomas Quasthoff, not to mention the conductors like Paavo Järvi, Esa-Pekka Salonen, or Yannick Nézet-Séguin—I'm afraid I can't name them all—it's clear that for Hélène Grimaud everything always boils down to the need, to the hope of "changing life," as Arthur Rimbaud said. In response to this, she never tires of saying that if a revolution should break out, it must address both the outer and inner worlds at the same time. She proposes nothing less than breaking down the barriers with which the antimonies of order oppose us: action and dream, man and woman, creation and preservation, tradition and innovation. She does this with a smile, sure of the victory that is assured to those who fight for all.

*Rebirth** can be seen from different angles. Hélène Grimaud wants her chosen title to be understood as "Renaissance," that period when art triumphed in Italy, the land of her parents's ancestors; but the renaissance she has in mind here, which we need now more than ever, this extremely singular artist warns us cannot take place without the prerequisite of a connection with our world in all its natural aspects. It is essential that we save it from the follies and degradations caused by the search for profit or the absence of heart. Hélène Grimaud takes as her own these words of writer Julien Gracq:

> The earth has lost its solidity and its foundation. Today, this hill can be razed at will, this river drained, these clouds dis-

*This book was originally published as *Renaître* (September 2023) which translates to "Rebirth."

> sipated. The moment is approaching when man will seriously face nothing but himself, and nothing but a world recast by his hand *to mirror his idea*—and I doubt that at that moment he will be able to rest to enjoy his work and say that his work was good.

To be reborn to oneself, to be reborn to others, to be reborn for common struggles, preserving *the otherness* of our relationship with our soul, since "I is another" as Rimbaud says, and to also be reborn to nature, which opens us up to infinity, is the path she illuminates in this book.

Stéphane Barsacq is a French writer, editor, and journalist known for his work in literature and cultural journalism, including notable interviews with figures like Pope John Paul II and Umberto Eco during his time at *Le Figaro Magazine*. The son of sculptor Goudji and grandson of playwright André Barsacq, he has authored essays on aesthetics, music, and spirituality, such as Johannes Brahms (2008), and his debut novel *Le Piano dans l'éducation des jeunes filles* (2016), which won the Roland de Jouvenel Prize. Barsacq has held key roles in publishing, including literary director at Éditions Robert Laffont and a position at Éditions Albin Michel, while living in Paris.

OVERTURE

Over the years I've been interviewed regularly by top journalists. They always helped me get a better handle on what I was trying to do; their attention helped me hear myself and sometimes understand myself better. I've also had interviews, offstage and backstage, with friends or colleagues who offered me the most precious thing of all: their time. Because it often takes time to get in tune with each other, to make one's voice heard, to distinguish the voice of the other, to see how they come across to us, and how we can respond to them.

Among these friends was Stéphane Barsacq, whose shared passion for literature and music, especially that of Johannes Brahms, whose biography he wrote, helped us form a strong bond. Incidentally I wrote the preface for it. Year after year, despite the ocean that separated us, we continued to talk, laugh, and dream, evoking the serious and the simple, the order of the day, where speech is composed of silence. Whether in Tokyo, Munich, Stockholm, Madrid, London, or Nantes, Stéphane always took notes after our conversations. One day he suggested that we publish them. I accepted but on one condition: that our conversations were transcribed and recast in the context of a book that would follow its own laws. I had in mind Béatrice Berlowitz's warnings at the beginning of her interviews with Vladimir Jankélévitch: "Nothing is more deceptive than recording; it's important to use it, but only to free yourself from it." Stéphane would send me questions and fragments, and I'd answer him, especially when I was on tour, where solitude can be both fruitful and inspiring. I began to enjoy this game more and more. There's nothing so fundamentally surprising about that. Isn't dialogue the most natural thing for a musician? Without this dialogue there is no music. It starts right away with the great musicians I interpret. I ask them how to understand a certain phrase, a certain phrasing, a certain intention, hidden or not. I ask them about the meaning of the score as it unfolds. The conversation that ensues allows the work to be played and responded to indefinitely. Other questions arise, and with them new insights. More generally, where would we be without this relationship with the other? Perhaps music begins with two? If we were alone, we wouldn't be able to sing, or sing with enthusiasm, because singing is a place of openness and sharing. A musician is always in dialogue with composers, with other musicians, and sometimes even with himself, in the most intimate part of his heart. Was it not St. Augustine who said: "I have become a question to myself"? And wasn't it Nietzsche who said that "love is a never-ending dialogue"?

But where to begin this book of conversations? The struggles around which my life crystallized? Yes, I want to talk about the creators of a music that holds meaning and that I can interpret. But I wanted to go far beyond what touches exclusively on the domain of music—even though, if you think about it, everything touches on music since joy, happiness, and the future itself are conjugated in relations to harmony. I wanted to speak to my sisters—by that I mean talk with women to tell them that being a woman is not a handicap if you have the desire to complete a project that is close to your heart. Being a woman is a question of constant rebirth, by seeing time not as an enemy but as an ally; where it is a question of being reborn to oneself, in a passion that is always clearer, more generous, and more hospitable. And what else? Life, of course, and to speak of it in the right tone—faith in all that it gives life to, faith in nature, which I have defended more precisely by taking the side of the wolves, as I am doing today in defense of the last wild horses. Live, and stop cursing life, as Rimbaud urges us to do. But what else? It was a little girl at the exit of a concert that gave me the inspiration I was still lacking. She simply asked me: "Music, what's the point?" For a brief moment, I was as dumbfounded as her parents. Yes, why make music? And why do all these musicians, thanks to whom we can hear a sound that crosses through the centuries, continue to do so? All these artists who neither produce nor manufacture anything in a world dedicated to matter and technology, a world where neither words nor dialogue are still really in tune with our exchanges. This book and the idea for its title in French, which when translated is "Rebirth," came about as a response to that little girl because I know that music is the word that comes to everyone's heart to express the paradise that is up to us—you me, everyone—to build here and now. The fact that music remains incorruptible, that it is the only language capable of crossing the density of time without ever failing to fulfill the vocation of all truth-telling; that of this Eden that it already lets us glimpse and that it re-enchants. That, like great music, there is no paradise unless it is replayed, as if it were created in the moment, beyond time. And finally,

Rebirth, because who will deny it is now urgent to recast the present and future, which have little or no use for life (or less and less use), and make man more and more deaf to music, precisely because it has the power to save him.

It's not enough to be born: it's important to return to the world, and to love it.

1

THE OCEANIC SENSE OF LIFE

Hélène Grimaud, you earned the praise of André Tubeuf, a friend of Elisabeth Schwarzkopf and Dietrich Fischer-Dieskau, a great musicographer in the tradition of Romain Rolland, and was, during his long life, a friend of the finest musicians from the creators of the operas of Richard Strauss to Rudolf Serkin. As a kind of lead in, with your permission, I would like to quote it. The portrait he painted of you makes an excellent starting point:

> *We didn't think so highly of her at first, a clean-cut, vivacious, beautiful girl and not ashamed of it, a post-sixty-eight girl who was born liberated and grew up free, we thought she was in a hurry because she's nimble, agile, and unencumbered. We thought she was a show-off because photography suits her naturally, and she's got fingers that make the spectacular look easy, such as Rachmaninoff or the superbly perilous Brahms. It took a long time for her to be accepted as someone who takes her time, and is contemplative and silent. In a dazzling polemic, written already a long time ago, Jean-François*

Revel stated, against all establishments, doctors, specialists, that a person will certainly not be a philosopher if he locks himself up in philosophy, closing himself off to everything else. Grimaud has opened things up. First the wide-open spaces. Thousands, perhaps millions, rushed in, or thought they were rushing in, with her. And then they bought one or two of her records. She opened something else with her writing. Spaces that are wide open in a very different way, landscapes with cypresses and cloisters. The castle of the soul.

Let's set the scene and start by talking about your landscapes, your landscapes by birth and your landscapes by choice. How important are they to you?

If you're going to paint a portrait, it's a good idea to start with the frame. There are so many people who are unhappy with their stay on earth! So many people who feel like strangers even in the places they frequent every day and never leave, except when they go on vacation. So many people who feel suffocated in cities and others who feel suffocated by boredom in the countryside. For me, landscapes and their contemplation have always been essential to keep my balance. I would define myself as *a citizen of the outside.* I can be satisfied with the minimum comfort of a house. I'm not afraid of living in a somewhat spartan home, with only the most essential furnishings. Perhaps it's because I've spent my life changing addresses, even countries, where sometimes I'm happy just to put down my bag without really moving in. I have to admit that between air travel and hotels, there's nothing to encourage me to enjoy a sedentary lifestyle. But scenery, the natural scenery! I can't go long without contemplating them or at least having their presence in my life. They are a vital need for me. First of all, it's from an aesthetic point of view. Some of them are the most beautiful and harmonious compositions of creation. Then I'm filled with gratitude and wonderfully calm. They reassure me. They restore my balance. Especially after the chaos of touring. I've never traveled as much as when I sit in my successive houses in South Salem, Switzerland, or in California, when I, into contemplation of nature with the idea—early in the morning—that the sun needs my presence in order to rise, where at the precise moment of its appearance, I would catch a glimpse of the universal secret by surprise—the mystery of the world would then be revealed to me. I've always enjoyed this game, when I'm alone, of unwinding my memories of trees and horizons, as well as clouds, like opening an album of postcards, or else constructing a landscape in my imagination where I could then stroll in the golden light of memory. Citizen of the outside, but sedentary vagabond! Everywhere in the world there's a little piece of Eden, as if Eden hadn't vanished but had been divided up and hidden in an infinite number of places that we discover during the course of our wanderings or by the happenstance of our personal destiny.

You asked me how important landscapes have been to me. I would say that early on I began using them as mirrors. Just as we discover our faces by looking at them, I discovered myself by looking at landscapes. They soothed my difficulties in socializing with other children and how that worried my parents. In nature, I finally felt that I'd found my place both in the universe and in the way I felt "centered again" within myself—with a sense of newfound harmony.

When I was a child, my mother used to recite poetry to me, and I remember this line that she almost hummed when she caught me by surprise in the car with my face glued to the window lost in contemplation of the fields and hills: "Your soul is a chosen landscape." For example, I have a precise memory of the moment when another specific landscape made me aware of my body and how it belongs to the earth. This was in Corsica, where I spent my vacations as a very young child with my parents. My mother was Corsican, a native of Olmo, a small mountain village. We would stay some hundred kilometers from there, not far from the sea, in Ghisonaccia to be exact. I used to sneak away on a path through the scrubland until the houses vanished from view. And I used to crouch down to avoid others seeing me and to give myself the illusion that I was alone in the world, closer to the ground, the ants, and the strongly aromatic wild plants. I used to then sniff the ground and listen with all my strength to the most imperceptible noises of nature. I was waiting, I didn't know what for, to smell the unique fragrance of this countryside—a fragrance that comes back to me sometimes and causes this whole memory to surge up. I would also bury my nose in the V-neck of my T-shirt and breathe in the warm smell of my own body, which would make me dizzy and finally convince me of my own existence.

Yet you spent your childhood in a city, a city that is also musical, because it is the site of a world-famous festival. It's where Balthus, who admired you quite a bit, as he has told me several times, worked on *Don Giovanni* in 1948 and on *Cosi fan tutte* in 1950. It's as if Mozart's music was already in the air before you were born . . .

Yes, I'm a native of Aix-en-Provence. All the same, I've never been a city kid. I feel rather strongly that the city is the most contrary and alien environment for childhood possible. There, a child has no opportunity to literally melt into her surroundings, to lie down in the grass, for example, and discover and observe shapes, colors, life—a blade of grass and the chirping of a cricket. To touch and even squeeze all these strange things: a leaf, grass, flower petals, a dewdrop, and even a spider, as well as the dirt she kneads so she can smell its aroma. The bizarrely shaped insects that I wanted to taste as a very young child, much to my mother's great displeasure. This experience is a little like a child's discovery of music when touching the instruments and hearing the sounds they make.

I think our urban lifestyle is terrible. Unfortunately, we rarely have, if ever, the possibility to choose. They cut the child off from the discovery of the seasons. The succession of these four beats imparts an unforgettable rhythm to the soul. Like a teacher, nature teaches the child the connections between his or her own emotions and the profound meaning of the transformation of creation: the sadness of autumn, the withdrawal and introspection of winter, the hope and joy of spring, and fulfillment and abundance of summer. It also initiates us into the mystery of time and its very essence, which, in short, is our own. It teaches us of death, but that it is a necessary stage of resurrection. Last winter, I was overwhelmed by the appearance of a violet under some snow crystals that I had scooped up to rub on my face. The grass was already pushing toward the sky with that powerful green color that makes spring so vibrant.

I remember everything that my wandering in nature has brought me. In its midst, in the heart of certain landscapes, I would find the deepest feeling of harmony with all that surrounded me. I would like to add that nature was the first and best school for me that I could ever imagine. I learned about power relations. There's an undeniable violence in nature, whether in the manifestations of the sky, storms, hurricanes, floods, or in the relationships between the links in the food chain. Horseflies on the rumps of horses, boring into them to drink their blood. The fox slaughtering a hen in a field. The hawk swooping down on a field mouse.

On the other hand, I never cease to be amazed by the resilience of flora, a resilience that is so often praised these days. In the most polluted industrial wastelands and the most inhospitable environments, in the cracks of the sidewalk or under the asphalt of small roads, its life force expresses itself with unheard-of tenacity.

As a city kid, I used to look at a blade of grass or a flower sprouting, or sometimes a tree getting established between the sidewalk and the pavement of a forsaken street, and it always moved me powerfully and lastingly. Again it was in nature that my first encounter, almost my apprenticeship, with death took place. I discovered its reality in the fly eaten by the spider in the middle of its web, the bird killed by a cat, or in the hedgehog run over on the road. And I understood all that this death gave birth to—the earth through the rotting of the corpse or the other species that it fed.

Finally, and most importantly, the landscapes gave me my first initiation into beauty and balance. Although it is the most perfect example of a truism, it's good to get excited by a sunset over the sea, or by the delicate balance of shapes and colors seen from the heights, or by admiring the inaccessible and mysterious peaks of a mountain range. But is there a more immediate access to beauty, one that gives that "oceanic feeling" of life that

Romain Rolland speaks about, than the landscape? Could we find a better way to educate the heart and the mind than to exercise the admiration it invites us to make?

I am constantly struck by the fact that I never see any flaw in the taste of nature, neither in color nor in form, nor even in the concert of its sounds—the tree frog and the owl, the bird and the wind. There are only sounds in nature while we make noise. A noise that is unbearable, a subject to which I will return. One day, by chance, I entered into an iris garden. It was unprecedented, those harmonies of blue and violet, white and pearl, those gradations and movements of leaves that responded to the curve of the petals and the sensuality of the pistils. It was evidence in that very moment that gave me an understanding of what perfection is.

I know how passionate you are about philosophy. You know that in the sixteenth century Spinoza drew a parallel between God and nature. He saw God in everything that exists and everything that exists in God. He didn't think God was content to create the world but that God was the world itself. From then on, human existence was determined by the laws of nature. Hence my questions: was beauty the only teaching that nature gave you?

It also gave me my first music lessons, long before I ever touched a keyboard. Of course, they were lessons by immersion, by occasional, furtive contact with the sounds bestowed by the elements. If the music that goes from Bach to Stravinsky by way of Brahms, Bartók, and Beethoven truly exalts the beauty of the world, of nature, and if it offers commentary on the themes of joy or sorrow, it's not just to please our ears. It is meant to convey that rare quality of emotional excitement we feel when the mind participates in the birth of life—and what better place to participate than nature? What better time for initiation than during childhood?

I remember that there was a large stone pine not far from where my parents live—nothing unusual about that in Provence. But the music it made when the wind blew and the modulations its branches made based on the nature of that wind—a simple breeze or a violent mistral—filled my ears. And what about the song of the cicadas, the song of the swifts in the Provencal summer sky, or the incomparable music of the great breath of the sea? These are so many melodies that an urban child can't enjoy. We used to live in a city that was relatively modest in size, though it's now part of a vast urban network surrounded by highways. But during my childhood, it was easy to get away from it. And in the city itself, we could go into neighborhoods that looked like they were in the countryside, places where nature had free rein to flourish.

It was during my walks, I should say my wanderings, that I first felt the temptation to sing alone and at the top of my lungs. I remember breaking into one of the songs that my mother used to hum while cooking. I especially remember one day when I ran away from school, and going home at an hour when the street was deserted, I felt so free that I was seized by an irresistible urge to sing. André Tubeuf, in his book on German song, says that this is the origin of the *lied*,* that song was born in the soul of a German wanderer who was walking around his farm along a

*German word for "song." In the Western tradition it refers specifically to an art song for voice and piano set to a German poetic text.

familiar stream and was moved by mist over a pond or by the nearby forest. So he began to sing, to express the sense of oneness he felt at that very moment when the beauty of his little corner of the world overwhelmed him. We can hear this hymn in Brahms's songs. This wanderer sang when he felt too far from his land to express all the regret he felt for leaving it and his desire to return. This ode can be heard again in the songs of Brahms, who wrote nothing else whose art was more pure or whose music was more accomplished. It's an intangible poetry, an imponderable substance without an atom of eloquence. Brahms celebrates a world in which everything is dialogue, in which everything listens and responds to each other, seeking the tension that resolves fears and anxieties.

Often when I'm walking with my dogs at my heels, I think about what André Tubeuf said and how right he was to suggest that when we walk in nature, taking human steps and treading gently, we are enrolled into the landscape. We enroll ourselves as if we were enrolled in school. Then it becomes impossible to feel the sense of absurdity that can sometimes seize us in life. Our own life and that of humanity in general on this earth. Moreover, I think that of all the lieder Brahms wrote, the one that maybe holds the general key is "Feldeinsamkeit," which tells us that when we lie down in the grass and watch the clouds drift by, we slowly and peacefully become one with death. Then the night is just another dream, like death, which is a friend.

In your evocation of nature and the lessons it has taught you, do you include your dogs, about whom you have spoken so often? The British philosopher Bertrand Russell had this to say last century, something that is more like a witticism than an absolute truth: "No matter how eloquently a dog may bark, he cannot tell you that his parents were poor but honest."*

It's not certain that you agree, I'm guessing. In any case, I believe you have several dogs today who are waiting for you and who accompany you when you wander through the woods.

My dogs, and my observations of their behavior, like that of other animals, have taught me more about human nature than any other experience or study. It may be what has given me the best view of it. They also remind me of my first inclination, before music captured me, to be a veterinarian or a biologist! I have always felt a real longing for the presence of animals, which is even stronger when it comes to wild animals, wolves and mustangs, and before them the horses of the Camargue since I had the privilege of getting close to them and letting them tame me. Both exert the same fascination on me. Their presence puts me into a trance, bathes me in occult currents, and summons me to the heart of a white hot, voluptuous world without lies, which I call my paradise lost. My playing has sometimes been influenced by the eyes of the gentle queen Alawa,† which pull me into the astronomical slope of another world. These animals, and my dogs when I follow them making their getaway into the middle of the enormous, dense forests of North America, when they force me to follow in their footsteps, to stop abruptly to catch the variations of the wind, to smell the scents that my footsteps release when walking on the dense earth and humus, bring me to the threshold of truly mythological revelations. I feel a strong desire when

*This quote is not documented; slight variations of it abound.

†A wolf-dog hybrid the author encountered in Tallahassee, Florida, and shared a special connection with.

I see them leaping in pursuit of an invisible prey, bursting out of the ferns with the powerful fluidity and kind of detachment only seen in wild animals. We will never exhaust the profound significance of animal metamorphosis in mythology and in the history of religions. From the World Serpent* to Ronsard's poem "Hymn to the Demons," in which we see the poet's terror of cats, the visible bodies of the Devil, and Faust's water dog; what a history of animals still remains to be written! Who will one day compile a poetic anthology, whose chapter on birds already exists thanks to the books by Jean de Bosschère? I dream of devoting whole pages to the horse! What a place it would hold as a catalyst of lyrical inspiration. Look at works of fantasy by painters and illustrators, all of whom have emphasized the terrible aspect of the horse, and of its skull. I'm thinking of Dürer, Delacroix, and Redon.

My dogs, and all the animals that I see in animal documentaries, which I can watch for hours, have put the word *fabulous* back at the top of my vocabulary. They force me to become aware of myself under the marvelous inner species of my animality. From hair to claw, from wing to beak, from snout to canine. And in the wandering of these thoughts, I rediscover a kind of ancestral memory. This abyss, between the animals and myself, sustains my passion for them. As for my dogs, their presence, always beautifully moving, is a never-ending source of joy, surprises, and discoveries. There is an understanding between them and me that I've never experienced with any human being. They have an additional quality that their presence offers me, like the one the wolves offer, and when I was a child, the horses

*From Norse mythology; a large and formidable serpent-like creature that lives in the sea.

that I admired in the Camargue—the possibility to change kingdoms—to enter into the natural, if not more accurately, the supernatural. When they look at me, they seem to know things about me that I don't yet know about myself. And their expression! It is one in which you can read love and the invisible. The expression of loyalty, something that is increasingly rare in the world, and increasingly opposed to man perhaps—and I don't exclude myself from the species. They are a pure expression of everything that makes us human and take me back to a state of innocence, of childhood, of the childhood of childhood.

One thing I'm proud of is that my country is the first one in the world to have created a dog cemetery, and I always invite the people I like to go visit it. I went there one November day when I was feeling a little sad. It is in Asnières-sur-Seine, on the island called "Ravageurs" that Eugène Sue gave a place of honor in his novel *Mysteries of Paris*. Ragpickers lived here until the end of the nineteenth century. A philanthropist, I dare say, but you have to love people in order to love those who love their dogs, bought it to create a dog cemetery there since a law had finally been passed allowing the burial of domestic animals on condition they were buried in a grave at least one hundred yards away from any dwelling and were at least one meter deep. In response, Georges Harmois and Marguerite Durand founded the Anonymous French Society of the Cemetery for Dogs and Other Domestic Animals. The cemetery opened at the end of summer that same year. It was divided into four sections: dogs, cats, birds, and the section for other animals, where many horse sculptures can be seen. I will always remember the emotion that filled my heart at the sight of these monuments, temples, garlands, and fresh flowers. The sight of these graves fills one with pity and sadness. The largest are the size of a small child and some are only the size of a human hand. In this strange place, deserted and full of flowers, cradled by the song of blackbirds and the cooing of pigeons, one phrase keeps coming back, one that sums up all the epitaphs, all the regrets, all the poems: "He was my only friend!" This is a cry of human loneliness at its poorest, most ephemeral, most commonplace, most irreparable. This is the silence that reigns over the island and the sculptures that dominate the mounds.

Was it during your walks that you began to think about writing? You recall the pages of Jean-Jacques Rousseau that are the preamble to Romantic literature in *The Reveries of a Solitary Walker.* Let me quote from it:

> *Having resolved to describe the habitual state of my soul, in the most unaccountable situation that ever mortal experienced, I can find no manner so simple and effectual, to execute this purpose, as to keep a faithful register of my solitary walks, and the reveries which accompany them; when I find my mind entirely free, and suffer my ideas to follow their bent, without resistance or control[.] These hours of solitude and meditation are the only ones in the day when I am entirely myself, and for myself, without diversion, or obstacle; and when I can truly say, I am what nature designed me.*

Yes, for as the body makes its way through the material plain of the natural world, the mind is thus liberated, free to roam the mountains and valleys of imagination unencumbered. It was during one of these walks, for example, that I imagined a short story, in the form of a uchronia.

Some men who had set out in search of the paradise they believed in so strongly found by chance the gate to the Garden of Eden and felt that their expedition was about to succeed. They pushed open the gate and went in. They shouted with joy and gazed in wonder at such beauty, the spacious skies, the luxuriant wild landscapes, but only in appearance, for the lions and giraffes, the wolves and lambs, all the fauna came out to greet them. They let the men approach and pet them. On the second day, Adam and Eve appeared. They were almost completely naked. They lived in a pretty teepee at the edge of a spring. The couple welcomed this small band. Adam and Eve invited the newcomers to sit down. They quenched their thirst. They let them taste fruits and dishes unfamiliar to these palates, which had suffered from hunger where they came from. They showed them how they lived—soberly and thereafter in peace and happiness. God provided for all their needs with his bountiful garden. That evening they prepared beds for their guests so they could rest.

On the third day, Adam and Eve showed them all the sights: plains, orchards, and hanging from a majestic tree, round, juicy, and golden, the Apple.

On the fourth day, the group got organized. They cut down the forests, killed the animals for pleasure or trade, and organized boxing matches because they were already at odds with each other.

On the fifth day, they stole the Apple and cut down the apple tree.

On the sixth day, Adam and Eve discovered that their tree was gone; they found the carcasses of the animals and saw the fighting over who would own the garden, its fruits and the

Apple. They didn't understand. Why kill? Why steal? Why take more than was necessary? They protested and asked their guests to leave the garden, go back to where they came from, and to leave them in peace.

At dawn on the seventh day, the small band, for once unanimous, had gathered together in front of Adam and Eve's teepee. They lifted up the woven leaves that served as a windbreak at the opening. Ten of them slipped inside.

And they killed Adam and Eve.

You just mentioned the role of nature in shaping your sensibility, but what about your "chosen landscapes"?

Ever since I was a child, I've had my heart set on a landscape. Unless that landscape chose me! That's exactly how I felt as a child: My parents and I left the city of Aix where I was born and where I spent my early years, until I left for Paris and the Conservatory.* That's where I discovered a landscape of birth and choice, at least the first one: The Camargue. I will remember this first encounter for the rest of my life. I knew, as I did later when I encountered the music of Brahms, that my life would never be quite the same because this landscape, like this composer, had responded to my expectations and concerns.

Both gave me a sense of fulfillment. After that first visit, I kept asking my parents to go back. When we went to the Camargue, for me it was more than just leaving the city, it was like entering a magical world. A dream that comes from the sea. I didn't immediately understand what it was about this

*The Paris Conservatoire/Paris Conservatory.

landscape that captivated me. I discovered it in Paris, in contrast to the completely mineral world of the city—without any of the Camargue escape routes Aix-en-Provence still allowed. Barely a few hours' drive away, we tipped over into another dimension where something wild and untamed triumphed violently. My emotions and attention, my anticipation, were so strong that I could mentally run through the whole route in all its details. Leaving Aix, arriving in Arles, leaving Arles, the route to Salins or to Saintes-Maries-de-la-Mer. I was tense like a bow. I scanned the landscape with all my might, impatient for the dirt road that would lead us into the secret nooks and crannies of the delta.

What did you feel then? Still that "oceanic feeling" of life?

If I'd felt like I didn't belong anywhere, here I felt invited to participate in a vast, harmonious order, fully invited and welcomed. I knew I was in touch with the elements in their rawest, truest, most primary form, as we say of colors, and I loved that idea. Water to begin with, whose beauty I would later seek out to express in music. There were these ponds and their mirrors as far as the eye could see, eventually embracing the Mediterranean and merging with it. There was the great, mighty river, the Rhone, which spread out in deltas as if, as it approached the sea, it multiplied in an intoxication of freedom, and that's exactly what I began to feel as the dream of being free, of living free, took hold of me. There was the sun, reflected as if the water had given birth to it, and the merciless glare of noon at the four cardinal points. Finally, there were the wild horses, whose beauty overwhelmed me. When startled, they would gallop away with a force that knocked me off my feet. The Camargue was much more for me than a landscape: it was a briefly glimpsed hint, a fleeting intuition of a harmony between my soul and a future. There, for the first time, I had a premonition of great things, of a destiny. If I am so committed to the preservation of wild mustangs, whose survival is threatened in the United States, I probably owe it to the deep joy I felt as a child whenever I saw these horses of the Camargue. They seemed to embody the wide open spaces and untamed nature of the region.

I also think I found myself in the Camargue as if in a mirror, because everything there is "too much": the sun is too biting, the wind too strong, the water too unpredictable. I allowed myself to be penetrated by the landscape, by the forms it has borrowed from living things. I felt myself as the horse, the mistral, the sun, the raging waves. I felt reconciled to my body, and friends with it. Neither girl nor boy, just a living being. That's how I would later feel with the wolves in the American far north. I have to also say that in my childhood, like in my adolescence, I was carried away by passion and the exaltation of discovery. The Camargue played on this string. It allowed me, more than anywhere else, to enter another universe that was, moreover, reserved for me, and to live each passing moment intensely. It was in the Camargue that I understood with every fiber of my being that I had to exist at the very edge of this encounter my presence was creating, between two eternities, the past and the future. It sharpened this gift that I had, that was revealed there and that I've kept, the gift of occupying the each second I live with all my strength. Perhaps it revealed my tendency to want to possess the elusive—the music of the wind and the sea, later that of the roar of fire, the crackle of ice in the Rockies, or the soft crunch of snow beneath my feet. I listened to them intently, taking them with me into my bedroom or to the corner of the schoolyard where I sought refuge during recess. When you think about it, the Camargue was probably my first music school and my first introduction to the secret pact I had decided to make with the animals in this unlikely land.

You seem to have a very vivid and precise memory of it.

Yes. Years later, my mother gave me a poem by Fernando Pessoa to read, and it proved to be a thunderbolt of meaning; its lightning rekindled my memory of that first encounter with horses in the lagoons of the Camargue and the copper light of the South:

> *I'm a keeper of flocks.*
> *The flock is my thoughts*
> *And my thoughts are all sensations.*
> *I think with my eyes and with my ears*
> *And with my hands and feet*
> *And with my nose and mouth.*
>
> *Thinking about a flower is when you see and*
> *smell it*
> *And eating a piece of fruit is when you know*
> *its meaning.*
>
> *That's why when on a hot day*
> *I feel sad from liking it so much,*
> *And I lie down lengthwise in the grass*
> *And shut my burning eyes,*

And when I feel my whole body lying in
reality,
I know the truth and it makes me happy.

I've reread this poem many times with the inexhaustible amazement of finding my own sensations and my own impressions written by someone else. On the beaches of the Camargue, in the forests of the far north with my wolves at night under the full, fat, fertile moon, lying full length in the vibrations of tall grass, I felt my whole body lying in reality. I knew the truth and it made me happy. When I heard one of Brahms's works played for the first time or when I surprised a student at the Conservatory deciphering one of his pieces, I felt the same sense of recognition. It was very strange. It's the feeling that something has been written for you, and that this something matches your emotional fluctuations perfectly. I felt like I was rediscovering these works even though I had never played nor even heard them before. I cannot shake this incredible feeling of familiarity, of something close to me, and made for me. The same thing was true about these verses. Of course I wanted to read the rest of this collection. How happy it made me to find these two lines, two poems later:

That lady has a piano.
It's pleasant, but it isn't the running of rivers
Or the murmur made by trees
Why does anyone need a piano?
It's better to have ears
And love Nature.

These verses sounded like a command, an order to leap beyond them. I told myself that I had to fill the space drawn by Fernando Pessoa, everywhere at work in nature, as in the music of living water, *legato, rubato,* elusive in its curves, whose musicality and elegance can never be said enough, but also in that of the wind, from the gentle song of warm breezes to the powerful whistle of stormy forests. My piano would have to cover the arc stretched between these wild sounds and their marvelous arrangement, as witnessed by the symphonies and concertos of Brahms, Beethoven's *Tempest* Sonata, and many other compositions. "Why does anyone need a piano?" Pessoa's keeper of the flock asks. To bring to the public the echo of flowing rivers, murmuring trees, and all the love that nature inspires. The thoughts inspired by this collection of poems—and those two in particular—led me to make recordings dedicated to water and to combine them during my concerts, with Mat Hennek's photographs of this vital element. From that reading, from that moment on, I wanted my piano to be the link between the public and its desire to reach the sky, the mountains, the oceans, the land of pure sounds, nature in its essence. I'm constantly trying to work on this quest, which sometimes becomes an obsession, at the risk, in the tension it demands, of sometimes breaking myself into a thousand pieces. But then, when I succeed in transcribing the fluidity and transparency of water, as I admired it as a child in the Camargue, and as a Debussy or a Liszt were able to capture, what a joy!

2

BETWEEN EUROPE AND THE UNITED STATES

You are known for your actions on defense of wolves. How do you explain this passion, which has nothing fake about it, as I can personally attest having seen it with my own eyes? Perhaps these words of a Romantic writer could be put in your mouth: "At forty, some turn bitter, others insipid; others turn into swine. I become a wolf. I say 'no,' I prowl and I remain unassailable in the great snowy woods."

Wolves are a constant source of fascination for us. Even I am still enthralled by their power. They bring out the savage in all of us. This is the source of some of their strength; the rest comes from the fact that they are superior to us. In their bodies, their fangs, on their loves, resides an elementary power similar to that of the wind, volcanoes, and the subterranean violence of life. In our midst, busy with our modest progression from one routine to the next, they come out of the snow of the Far North and the red hues of autumn to ensure the wild domination, the cold and solemn ferocity of nature. Each time they appear, from the Russian steppes to the Canadian forests, from the Spanish sierras to the Aubrac plateau, where, it seems, two individual wolves have just been discovered, they give us the unique possibility to catch a glimpse of a vision: the intuition of the truth. This truth deep within our consciousness is what allows each of us to draw from within the forces of creation—for me, to find the joy that makes me play Brahms or Rachmaninoff.

"I believe . . . That the borders of our mind are ever shifting," William Butler Yeats wrote, "and that many minds can flow into one another, as it were, and create or reveal a single mind, a single energy. That the borders of our memories are as shifting, and that our memories are a part of one great memory, the memory of Nature herself." Following in his footsteps I can affirm that wolves are that memory, a living remnant of Eden. Wolves do more than talk to us, they give us answers. What questions do they answer? Only those that are essential for our future: How can we save the planet? How can we save our children? Some four hundred thousand scientists—anthropologists, ethnologists, ecologists, biologists, economists—have submitted a report to the United Nations on the state of the Earth. Their conclusions are alarming and unanimous: If humans don't respect each ecosystem and bring them all into balance, the world will be uninhabitable in thirty years. Studies of wolves in Yellowstone Park have shown how essential the presence of this most noble of predators remains for the balance of this ecosystem. The wolf reminds us of our origins. It reminds us that our ancestors needed animals to survive in nature. The adventure of this complicity began with wolves, through mutual observation and patient taming. The wolf taught our ancestors how to hunt, then he helped them to catch food. It taught them the importance of economy and respect for others—to kill only when necessary and only those individuals who are the least essential to the survival of the group. The rules of life in the pack taught man the rules of life in society. The women of some peoples nursed young wolves to seal this alliance. Some gods have adopted them as brothers: Apollo made the wolf his symbol. Mars entrusted wolves with the task of drawing his chariot while the two founders of Rome owed their survival to them.

Today, on this Earth where mankind is committing a massive genocide of all life—where dozens of animal and plant species disappear every day—where 16,125 new species are threatened with extinction in whose ranks, newly designated after the polar bear, we find the hippopotamus, we must state loud and clear that the wolf is the future of humanity. This ancient partner, which no great civilization has failed to consecrate in its legends, will live only if we live. Or rather, we can only survive if we protect it, but not in reserves or sanctuaries. No ecosystem can be isolated from others, as the latest United Nations report rightly pointed out. We must give wolves the space and life they rightfully deserve, so that our children can be assured of having the land and oxygen they rightfully deserve. In this way, the old philosophical debate—long based on the observation of wolf pups—finds a new field of reflection. Where is the line between man and animal? This question, which passionately stirred the Church, then the Enlightenment, and inspired the greatest thinkers such as Descartes or Kant, has found, in ecology or ethology, if not an answer, at least an observation: Both are alive, and cannot remain so without each other. Hurricanes, earthquakes, tsunamis, the melting of the ice caps, the depletion of fresh water:

These are the facts that now translate into thousands of human deaths. Scientists and economists are beginning to hear the call of the Earth. In addition to economic calculations of profitability, market prices and management issues, they recognize their duty to integrate a new parameter: the preservation of nature. Where can this be studied? In what schools? As our ancestors did two million years ago, let's look at wolves. Let's really look at wolves. Often hated, sadly hunted, they continue, in the absolute freedom of their runs and loves, to teach us that meaning which eludes us, which frightens us and yet which we hear on certain moonlit nights, when they howl at the sky: paradise is here, *there where they are.*

Let's go back to your youth in Provence. If you loved this countryside so much, why did you leave it? Why did you go to America? You had all you needed to live happily in France. At the age of thirteen, you were unanimously awarded first prize at the Paris Conservatory. Your first record playing Rachmaninoff won an award. Famous conductors wanted to help further your career. Why did you leave at such a young age—at nineteen?

To tell the truth, it took me a long time to understand what had prompted my desire to leave France, then to build, and finally to affirm. But I wasn't running away from anything. Neither longing, nor heartache, nor the slightest restriction of any kind. I went *elsewhere* not in search of what I couldn't find in Europe at the time, but for what I couldn't define at that point in my life. Something beyond the magnificent love of my parents. A freedom perhaps . . . a *key.*

My encounter with the plight of and relationship between

wolves and humanity, and the decision to protect them, along with my chance encounter with Alawa, led me to stay in the United States. Many theories have been put forward about my fondness for these animals and the fact that for years I dedicated myself entirely to their preservation—not counting the time devoted to music, but music has never been an activity or a profession for me, it was and still is a part of me. It has been suggested that the wolves were just a way to stir up old emotions that lived in me as a child, like all children, but in an acute way: fear and the desire to kill, coupled with fear and the desire to be killed. Someone wrote that there was no need to read Freud's *Wolf Man* to be gripped by the bond that unites the ferocity of the male wolf with the sensuality of the female wolf. But who wondered what the truth was, and had become during my meeting with Alawa, which owed everything to chance? Was it really coincidence, or was it the meeting with my destiny? Why did I feel the need to go out one evening in Florida and walk randomly through the labyrinth of houses and streets of that city? I will never forget the moment when my eyes met those of that fabulous animal, this she-wolf. It was as if an electric charge ran through my whole body. Contrary to her habits, she let me slowly approach her. A meeting. A "recognition." One of those pivotal moments of life we all experience, more or less intensely, when I knew that my life would be changed forever. The chances that a young French woman would be in Tallahassee, Florida at that very moment were so slim! I believe there is a reason for everything, and it's as if everything conspired to make that meeting happen that night, and it happened so that later would be born the Center for the Protection of Wolves, which I founded near New York City, and for which Alawa was the ambassador, would be born. This is what drove me to settle in the United States. I stayed on the other side of the Atlantic to devote myself seriously to the study of these animals. As one of my childhood aspirations was to become a veterinarian, something my career as a concert pianist left me little time for, I enrolled in some animal behavior courses. In fact, I'm still toying with the idea of writing a book about my observations over the years. In other words, that first encounter was primarily a catalyst, but by no means a decisive factor. I had never been fascinated by wolves before. The fascination came later, by force of circumstance. All things considered, I would have chosen to study the primates of Borneo. I got permission from the government to keep wolves permanently, as ambassadors for their species. I then continued my research with them, while inviting school groups to interact with them. When I ran the center full time, I wanted to teach children about these animals through direct contact, and to teach them to respect the ecosystem. To tell the truth, I'm still amazed to see that little ones have a greater intuition of what's essential than adults.

Thanks to wolves, I also learned much more about myself. They allowed me to confront love with death, that two-sided drama of eternity and nothingness. Who has realized how much their presence, the presence of the essence of nature that they embody, emphasizes what music offers: the very condition of possible access for everyone to metaphysical experience? The wolves and the music founded this "I" that is all beings and that fascinates history with the metaphorical energy of harmony. The wolves, associated with music, held for me—and this is still true today—certain secrets of abundance; they brought me into the intimacy of things, they integrated my various expectations. In fact, wolves have given me a kind of serenity; they don't allow any deception. They call for a heightened level of emotion, sincerity, and commitment that has nourished my playing and continues to do so. Music and wolves? In fact, they both guard ancient secrets that are more relevant now than ever.

What has your American exile brought you, an experience you share with Sergei Rachmaninoff, Igor Stravinsky, and Arnold Schoenberg? Especially since you courageously left everything behind. It is true that you had already spent your entire adolescence far away from home studying at the National Conservatory in Paris and not in Aix-en-Provence, to which you only returned on weekends?

I have felt out of place since childhood. I didn't feel any more at home in Aix than in France, despite my origins. After my years in Paris, I wanted to start all over again, both as a pianist and as a human being. The experience of anonymity was indispensable. It was the price of my rebirth: I needed solitude. Why the United States? As I already told you, coincidence (my introduction to wolves and all they represent, along with my chance meeting with Alawa) played a role in this as I already told you, then I used this aphorism, which I believe is by the poet Edmond Jabès: "If you don't know your way, ask someone like you who is looking for it." Over there, especially in New York, I met a lot of artists my age who were also looking for something. Like me, they had come to cross swords with the roughest and most ruthless opponent in order to hone their calling. New York has little room for amateurs and even less for fakes. When it comes to work of any kind, Americans have one invaluable quality: their open-mindedness. They exhibit an intelligent practical ability to judge work on its merit and not by the person who supports it or the commentary that may be made about it. We value talent, not the person who expresses it.

Would you say that you have changed?

Yes and no. I've never been a fan of half-measures, but after all the experiences I have had from exile, solitude, and the creation of the Center, to getting used to performing on stage, I think I've found a balance, without moderating my passions in any way. After all the years I've spent on this continent, I see things differently. I love France more than before, maybe because I've become a foreigner there. And there are some unpleasant aspects of the United States, but they have not contaminated me. There's no point in arguing. On the one hand, I've grown accustomed to two things that are hard to find elsewhere, and which I miss very quickly when I'm away too long. One is the genuine friendliness of people. Americans can be a little naive—they are still pioneers—and they have a spontaneity I like, something I still find more in women. It's that little bit of swagger, that special form of courage and daring that is crystallized and embodied by heroines like Amelia Earhart, the first woman to cross the Atlantic in her small plane, who mysteriously disappeared at sea, or like my inspiration, Dian Fossey, who has dedicated her life to protecting and preserving gorillas. But what I also like in America are the wide-open spaces that still exist all over the country, and that they are part of American culture and education—immersion in these vast spaces is part of the school curriculum. The summer camps, that Hollywood has often given us a glimpse of, pitch their tents in the middle of the great national parks where the wild world, in the noble sense of the word, still finds a way to continue. I like these spaces, where the cancerous presence of man has not yet spread, with every fiber of my being. Nature unfolds there, gives itself a future, and I feel at home. I feel reassured. It's in some of these worlds that I have experienced extremely powerful, almost violent, feelings, comparable to those that music bestows upon me.

You are describing a precise feeling that those who listen to you often feel, especially at one of your concerts. It's the impression that this world is connected to another world, usually invisible, but whose presence, once you reveal it, can probably save us, but what feeling do you want to talk about?

During the pandemic, I had to drive across the United States from California to South Salem, on the East Coast. From the Southwest to the Northeast. During this trip, I took the opportunity to go for a walk—alone but with my two dogs—in Bryce Canyon in southern Utah, a place that inspired a work by Olivier Messiaen, *Des Canyons aux étoiles.** With a map of the area and possible hikes in hand, I set off at a brisk pace, my dogs hot on my heels, to make the most of the wonders and panoramic views of the region. Despite the relatively late hour, nobody else had yet ventured out on the paths. I had chosen to follow the Navajo and Queens Garden trails based on the recommendations of the tourist brochure—two or three hours of hiking, all uphill. It was chilly. The air was filled with the fragrance of pine trees

**From Canyons to the Stars.*

and the subtle scent of melted snow and soaked herbs. Soon I entered a labyrinth, and after a long hike I reached the site.

It is impossible to describe the feelings that this natural theater can evoke in a visitor who has not prepared for it. It's not strictly speaking a canyon, like the ones I've seen from an airplane window, or admired in movies or ads—the very famous views of dizzying cliffs overlooking the Colorado River. No, it was a vast explosion of the terrain overlooking the trail I'd ventured onto, where thousands of rock needles, blood red, pink, ochre, and orange, rose into the sky. They literally seemed to crackle, interrupted in places by the sharp cones of tall firs. This gigantic field of stalagmites was hollowed out here and there by deeper ravines; wind, ice, sand, and especially time had hollowed out and sculpted the rock, creating these dizzying spires.

Clinging to the cliffs, they built chimneys so fantastic, so unheard-of, that they seemed to be the work of the fairies whose name they bore. I never tired of admiring these "hoodoos" that pierced the intense, deep, almost sea-blue air. I immediately understood why Messiaen had chosen this title, *From Canyons to the Stars,* and wanted this work to be "geological and astronomical, a score of colors," saturated with hues and shades whose infinite subtlety appeared before me. What other landscape could illustrate, symbolize, and practically embody the birth of hopes and promises, the fresh novelty of this land hitherto unknown to the waves of immigrants from such an old Europe?

I remained there, motionless, for almost an hour, looking with all my strength. There wasn't a sound except for the wind blowing through the pipes of those mineral organs and, more faintly, the concert of birds that Messiaen had invited into his work. This setting, like the score, had an overwhelming mystical dimension. The landscape seemed to tremble, not from erosion, but from constant intrusion, as if at the heart of a genesis swept by the ardor of the sun, now high in an unchanging sky. I was reminded of Paul Gauguin's words: "I believe that the faithful disciples of great art will be glorified and that—enveloped in a celestial tissue of rays, of perfumes, of melodious sounds—they will lose themselves forever in the bosom of the divine source of all Harmony." I was right there. It was then that my chest swelled with a powerful, almost painful emotion that was almost a sob.

You've become an icon of classical music from Tokyo to Stockholm, but many people associate you with wolves. Is this a burden to you, a marketing fact, or just the price of fame these days?

Nothing to do with marketing, believe me! I have never pretended to be a zoologist to attract attention. The center I created requires working in a wild environment every day. It is a lifestyle that is radically different from show business. It's just like being a performer. You don't marry wolves or music to become famous. Your comment reminds me of a very cruel passage from *Madame Bovary*: "She gave up playing the piano. Why practice? Who would ever hear her? Since she would never play for an audience, in a short-sleeved velvet dress, on an Érard piano, skimming over the ivory keys with the lightest of fingers, never feel a murmur of ecstasy rising about her, what was the point of practicing any more?"

The audience is never fooled about my intentions. I have never heard the slightest doubt expressed in this regard. But it is undeniable that the wolves have drawn some elements of my audience to me, and that gives me great joy! And who cares about my critics! That's a risk you have to take. You won't commit to a cause if you tremble at the thought of exposure or worry about what people will say. Whenever it's possible to help raise awareness among as many people as possible, it's important to do so, especially when it comes to defending the environment. As far as the comments that these actions might inspire, some slip-ups are inevitable. Besides, I am very happy that my fame as a musician allows me to defend this cause that is so close to my heart. I am able to correct misconceptions, and at my humble level, participate in a mission that should concern and motivate us all, the respect of the flora and fauna, in other words the survival of the planet. To kill wolves with impunity is to say that everything is possible through barbarism. It's with this kind of violence that man, by demonizing animals, has given himself the luxury of destroying our mother's house, the Earth in a blind, insane race to self-destruction. As Marguerite Yourcenar writes: "Man is unlikely to cease being a *torturer* for man, as long as he continues to learn his trade as an *executioner* from the beast." I've felt this feeling of revolt since I was a child; it still fills me and I want to believe that we can change the course of this rampage. That's what I want to devote myself to, and I'll be happy if this dual facet of my work—nature conservation and music—raises public awareness of both. The posterity of my foundation is a great reward. Today, it has more than four-and-a-half-million followers.

Yet, one day, in the middle of the 2000s, you left the United States and your wolves to move to Europe, between Berlin, Germany, and Lake Lucerne in Switzerland, where Rachmaninoff

once stayed. It is true that these countries have a strong musical tradition?

When I began an international career, I had less and less time to devote to the Wolf Conservation Center. I delegated a lot of responsibilities to professionals, including managing the site. I told myself that I would dedicate myself to music, and I returned to Europe. But something broke in my inner balance. I rediscovered the strange feeling of personal dissatisfaction. I worked on other pieces, I rehearsed, I went on concert tours. But this time I was feeling an almost compulsive need to meet the public. Maybe it was the need for a greater form of love. I believe that love starts with deep compassion, transported by deep emotion: a revelation within and without that carries meaning within the measure of each individual. If there is a key word in love, perhaps it is this: compassion. Compassion? I mean to take in the suffering of others, to give them all one's tenderness in order to restore their joy in the pure wonder of being. And it was with the audience that this secret desire could be fulfilled. It was a sensual, almost carnal desire. The piano is sexual like us; its rebellion, nostalgia, affinities, and tendencies are magnetized like ours by the archetype of the androgyne. They obey a higher eroticism whose music promotes decisions and countershocks, dramas and resolutions; music opens a space for all adventures, all miracles. In music, as in love, body and soul are one. What the body wants, the soul wants too; where the body clings, the soul clings, and both go together to wherever desire calls them; the lower part forms the pedestal that serves as the foundation for the higher part. Finally, I wanted to feel to my heart's content the truth that every pianist discovers sooner or later: music only really begins with the listener, starting from the moment it enters the warmth of the heart and secretly inhabits its silence. A musician—for me a man like Serkin—is only as great as the greatness he reveals in his fellow man.

Why, after this European interlude, did you return to the United States, where, it's true, there are great orchestras?

For ecological reasons. I felt the need to reinvest myself in the fight to conserve nature and help endangered animals to survive. In a strange way, working on Brahms's Second Concerto, far away from Salem where I lived in the United States and where I had founded the Wolf Conservation Center, made me realize that the various spheres of my activities that I had thought separate were actually deeply connected. Music and wolves, writing and ecology. Ignoring the fate of all the living things we disfigure—animal or plant species—left me feeling incomplete. In fact, none of this struggle was really over, nor would it ever be, especially if I threw in the towel along the way. You can't live without music, but you can't live on music alone. This struggle is also what Mat, my companion, was committed to in his photographic work—these correspondences between music and the elements, between sound and water in its most primordial form. Where else, if not in the United States, could we find suitable material for our actions? Such actions are becoming increasingly necessary, as we have been reminded by the outbreak of a virus capable of paralyzing an economy on a global scale, a virus about which the hypothesis we know very little except to identify it with images from China. Its appearance reminded me of that of SARS.* In my book, *Return to Salem,* I imagined and hypothesized a correlation between the devastation of the planet and the appearance of this bird flu, which had already frightened us when people in China reported dying from this new disease transmitted from the animal kingdom. This correlation has since been verified. It still hasn't brought about an end to deforestation or the abuse of the last remaining large nature sanctuaries. Nothing has been done to step on the brakes of global warming. The ice pack continues to melt and the major powers speed up the phenomenon so they can explore and mine the ground that will be exposed by the disappearance of the ice as well as the permafrost, which we know is full of unknown germs and viruses. We can no longer remain silent or rely on the authorities to do anything. That's why I came back to the United States without being forced to do anything. I'm happy here. I love America and, as you can imagine, its wide-open spaces—the exhilaration of space that you can feel there.

Was *Return to Salem* a novel or an autobiography?

In Hamburg, where she is rehearsing Brahms's difficult and torturous Concerto No. 2, the narrator finds herself by chance in the strange warehouse of an antiquarian. There she buys a manuscript illustrated with engravings and musical scores, a mirror that may have belonged to Lewis Carroll, and a small golden key. She quickly discovers that the manuscripts are signed with a pseudonym Johannes Brahms liked to use, and that the engravings, signed by the famous German engraver

*Severe Acute Respiratory Syndrome.

Max Klinger, are dedicated to the composer. Everything—the mirrors, the engravings, the stories—evokes a fantastic, disturbing universe. She had these pages translated, which evoke a journey to a place described as the Garden of Eden, but a garden in ruins, plunged into absolute silence and haunted by ghosts. The difficult German translation came to her in bits and pieces and the narrator, increasingly intrigued by the story's analogies with the current state of the planet—the extinction of species, global warming occurring much more rapidly than even the most catastrophic scenarios had predicted, human deafness to the ecological peril, the massacre of wolves and bears—decided to search in Brahms's life what might have inspired it. Had he really made this journey? Or were these stories that he heard from his confidant, Robert Schumann? Schumann went mad, and from his asylum he never stopped evoking silence, unheard-of music, ghosts, angels and red demons. Robert Schumann was in contact with Chamisso, a writer and botanist who went on an expedition to the North Sea, which is also the setting of Johannes Brahams's story. Had they all discovered the Other World, whose principle the Romantics defended, a parallel world like that whose existence is defended today in quantum physics? The narrator investigates, and the more she investigates, the more the story absorbs her, showing her that she, too, is part of it. It's as if none of the choices she made were by chance but, on the contrary, long foreseen. It's as if, through the play of doubles, of mirrors, from Schumann to Clara, from Brahms to Hugo Wolf, from the works that had been composed to those she performed, she was charged with a destiny. But which one? She finally found out that the journey described by Brahms, if it happened, must have been the one he made to the island of

Rügen in northern Germany, a major place in German mythology. There, she learned that music alone was not enough for her life. She had to return to Salem to resume her fight; to alert people to the apocalypse threatening the Earth, about which very few individuals actually cared as shown by the impoverished nature of the most recent summits on the subject, to lend her voice to the struggles to defend endangered species, and to spread ecological awareness through music, which is closely connected to the conservation of a world made for human beings. In Rügen she realized that the Garden of Eden was nothing but the Earth, from which humanity exiles itself every day, and that Hell is only a destroyed paradise inhabited by ghosts of animals slaughtered into extinction, and infected by the poisons we pour into it in greater quantities every day. So she returns to Salem to fight for her wolves, who are now being hunted all over the world, and she is determined more than ever to embody, with force, the vision and message of the Romantics—the last to see the beauty of nature and art as fundamental principles of progress, and as the only possibilities for the future. It's up to you to decide whether it's a novel or not!

So there is not a single city that you have conquered whose landscape carries a special meaning for you? Even if it is true, as Baudelaire says in "The Swan" that "the shape of a city / alas, changes more quickly, than the heart of a mortal." It should be noted that Baudelaire saw this as a sign of modernity.

Today, I love rediscovering Paris and strolling through it with my mother. But how I hated this city when I was at the Conservatory, and in the years that followed. The days were so short! The nights were so long! Light was rare there and the lamps were lit in the middle of the afternoon. When you got up, it was dark out. The day had barely begun and it was already over. Paris seemed to be like a theater of fate to me: a thousand stages were open opposite each other and everyone was performing, everyone for everyone and everyone for no one. The streets were the backstage and all the passersby walking through them in every direction strangely knew their roles. More than ever, life looked like a sad and haunted comedy. It's true that urban landscapes didn't move me at all at that time. It's not that I found them particularly ugly. There are even beautiful ones, or more precisely strange ones, like New York.

In fact it's thanks to New York that I began to look at cities and sometimes to love them. I love this city because I believe it's where the heartbeat of America can be found in everything this megalopolis offers in the way of movement, the promise of freedom, and success to individuals who have come to try their luck. I will remember for the rest of my life the shock of seeing it for the first time. It was after Tallahassee, a small city in the middle of nowhere in Florida. I had landed there when I was nineteen and spent some time there, and—as you know—that's where I met Alawa, my first wolf. When I left Florida, I moved to New York. It was in New York that I was able to harness the energy that ended the trial of extreme loneliness that I had faced during my first stay in America. I took what it had to give me, which was very healthy for me at the time, and I took a deep breath before I migrated north to live with the wolves—something like a powerful electric current ran through me, a lesson in courage and determination to not give up on myself or my dreams. This is a rule that the majority of New Yorkers live by and live under. In truth, New York defies the very notion of a city. The scale is altered. Nothing is ever repeated, but everything remains unchanged, and everything is reduced to one intense activity: making the city exist by existing oneself with the utmost intensity. New York forces us to rethink all orders in a dizzying intoxication.

There was one more reason for my affinity with this megalopolis—I could connect it to music, to a sound, George Gershwin's *Rhapsody in Blue.* Rarely has there been such perfect match of music and place, and of this place with an era that witnessed the emergence of promises of renewal and a land of innocence, earthly happiness, and freedom—so many elements that drew me to this city and gave me a lasting connection to its spaces. Wherever this *Rhapsody* is played, New York looms up in the imagination. During that first visit, I couldn't help but think of my colleagues, not to mention my co-religionists, those jazz musicians who had landed in the Big Apple, an apple as big as stage fright clutching their throats, to say with their brass and percussion what the sufferings and joys of their sisters and brothers of color, but also of all human beings, inspired in their music—that famous and incomparable "blue note." "A pianist is an architect who uses rhythm as his basic material," Leon Fleisher taught me during a memorable master class. This is what the tightrope walkers of jazz also realized when they held all the variations of a theme in the same stave.

I still believe that New York's beauty stems from the symbols that its architecture defines and that sum up the expectations of the intrepid people who set out for this city, their hearts filled with desire. The ever-higher skyscrapers could just as well be called cloud piercers. Then there are the magnificent bridges that span opposing shores both connecting and marking the distance between Manhattan and the rest of the continent, and with the rest of the world. Among these bridges, including that of Manhattan, Williamsburg, and Queensboro, there is of course the Brooklyn Bridge whose upper level I loved to cross from the beginning and which the intense traffic of cars and trucks makes it vibrate "like a lyre," as Paul Morand noted. There is more music in the melodious wail of ferry and boat sirens as they glide along the banks of the Hudson, one hundred and sixty-five feet below. When the tide rolls in, the Atlantic pushes its currents and storms their swells. Lastly, New York doesn't resemble any of the other cities in the United States that all look alike. It's only in New York that I feel American. And South Salem with the wolves is where I feel completely at home.

3

INITIATIONS

You told me one day that your mother had passed on to you her passion for Paul Cézanne, your Aix compatriot, of whom Rainer Maria Rilke, someone else dear to you, wrote: "His still lives are miraculously absorbed into themselves." Was your sensitivity to art awoken when you were a child?

Yes, and it's a gift of chance the value of which I realize a little more every day. I thank my parents for this; they were lovers of literature and music, but also of the arts in general. It's true they were both teachers and I benefited from their natural tendency to learn and teach. Discussions at home revolved mainly around aesthetic issues and the illustrated books my father regularly brought home. I learned them by heart with an all-consuming passion for the pictures. Books were my first friends before music. My parents' library was a treasure chest. They always had great taste. They taught me that there is no other intelligence than to pay homage to the beauty of the world, to participate in it with love, and to add the gift of oneself. That's when you create and become an object of creation for yourself.

They introduced me to Paul Cézanne, a native of Aix-en-Provence in fact, when we went for a walk in the direction of Sainte-Victoire.* But even more, they taught me to love Italy and its artists from Giotto to Leonardo, from Masolino to Brunelleschi, and all those whom an inventory at Le Prévert would not include, Masaccio, Simone Martini, and Paolo Uccello, who I discovered later in the work of Antonin Artaud and, perhaps my favorite, Sandro Botticelli—I still remember the day when I learned that his name means "little barrel"! What could connect this artist—who I imagine to be as handsome as his heroes of antiquity—with a little barrel? I also remember the day when my mother showed me that the throat and hips of Botticelli's Venus were not human. I tried to imagine myself like that in everyday life and, conversely, I tried to imagine my teacher with the dimensions of the goddess. These were games in which reality and imagination were equal, and in which humor and reverie played a large role. What's more, I've sometimes had the physical impression that the holy halos that can be seen in the Assisi frescoes were truly the expression of divine essence.

Was this initiation later "useful" in your musical education? We know that painters and musician have ties, like that between Picasso and Satie, just as there are musicians who are also painters like Mikalojus Konstantinas Čiurlionis or Arnold Schoenberg. On the other hand, what painter hasn't painted musicians? From the angels on the cathedrals to the very mysterious ones of Paul Klee . . .

---

*Mountain ridge in the south of France.

It's impossible to play Schumann's music and not cross paths with Caspar David Friedrich. Similarly it is impossible to perform Frédéric Chopin and not like Eugène Delacroix, especially when we know of their lifelong friendship. It's impossible to even listen to Brahms without seeing Max Klinger's watercolors. Ravel, Debussy, or Stravinsky had close ties with Bakst, Picasso, or Chagall. When I was younger, I went through a Vincent Van Gogh period; a man who suffered alone, but who triumphed over his suffering, the creator of a radical work that turned our vision of the sun upside down.

I now think he and his sunflowers look alike. I also have a passion for everything that has to do with the human face. How can I not be truly "stunned" by the portraits of Fayoum, Rembrandt, or Francis Bacon, despite their lack of beauty, but of an even deeper connection to beauty? Mark Rothko's paintings also move me: secular icons dedicated to rhythm.

And do you have any favorites outside of painting?

I have great admiration for Frank Gehry, the architect of the Guggenheim Museum in Bilbao, Spain. He created a concert hall in Los Angeles and I played there for the opening. It's a marvel. Otherwise, my profession has given me the good fortune to work with photographers like Sarah Moon, Annie Leibowitz, and James Nachtwey. They are also artists whose eyes have the integrity of a compass. And how could we miss the connection between music and the visual arts? In both cases, it involves a reading of the outer form. The painter is the one who sees, the musician is the one who hears. Of the painter is a genius, the appearance he paints tends to be better than a copy of reality: its appearance. Painter, sculptor, musician, the differences scarcely matter. Every painter, unless he is lying, has only one goal: to unveil the world, to make it appear, to give it its tragic beauty. I'm moved by this power, and it connects me to certain artists in whose work I've witnessed this alchemy, this unveiling, in different fields. Some filmmakers, for example, are true plastic poets; I'm thinking of Ingmar Bergman, Emir Kusturica, and Quentin Tarantino. Otherwise, I'm particularly fond of the work of some living creators, like Goudji, the inventor of a sacred universe, rich in myths, animated by the search for a lost time, but also for a time to come. I still appreciate the works of Gerhard Richter, the works in Indian ink of Gao Xingjian, or the works of Augustin Frison-Roche.

An artist who I still admire today is Balthus. I learned that he had died when I was in New York. I immediately raced to the Metropolitan.* I collected my thoughts in front of one of my favorite paintings: his *La montagne*. I was very touched by the fact that this great painter had let me know of his support for the creation of my center since 1988. I had the impression that Balthus had become all his characters, that he had joined his beloved Rainer Maria Rilke, who had raised him, and the day was beautiful.

You owe all this to your parents? Proof that the only child who is open is the one who has been offered that opening, that release to horizons other than those of necessity or, all too often, those of violence.

*Metropolitan Museum of Art.

They gave me the key. They made me realize very early on that in artistic matters it's not a matter of proving, but of moving and convincing. Hence the concept of tact, in every sense of the word. A tact that never diminishes or disappears. I think it's the "living greats" like Beethoven or Rachmaninoff, or the painters I've just mentioned, among many others, who, even when they're dead, rule our lives on borrowed time. If I placed my book *Private Lessons* in Italy, it was to pay homage to my parents' Italian heritage, and to our travels there when I was a child.

In this book, I wanted to tell the story of an imaginary trip—a journey through space and an inner journey—undertaken to heal my dissatisfaction with life and music; a return to my ancestral land, Italy, into the depths of my own culture, conversations with the strange characters fate had thrown on my path, answers to essential questions that I had buried in my memory; all this would bring me the key that I had lost, the key that would reopen the door to desire, to exchange, and to enthusiasm, and finally to music in all its invigorating urgency. The old Collector who I meet in this book, or Beatrice in the clutter of a garden, taught me, as I had learned from my parents, to listen to the great music of the Earth, the breath of the Ocean, the moans of the Rock, or those of all the frightened fauna. Communion with the elements, meditation where the sky opens, symbiosis with the whole of nature.

Did Italy play a role in the formation of your artistic taste? I remember walking with you in Rome. We had gone to see the statue of Marcus Aurelius, the philosopher-emperor, about whom Pierre Hadot wrote that he strove to practice three fundamental disciplines: "to see reality as it is by freeing himself of all prejudice born of passion, to accept with love the events that arise from the general course of Nature, and to act in service to the human community." Then we went to the Ponte Sant'Angelo* where the angels form a hedge of honor, then you introduced me to the Trastevere . . .†

Italy is the land of beauty, of all contrasts, of the sweet life as cultivated in Rome or Florence, and of a certain asceticism, as in Umbria or Apulia. Everywhere seems to be inhabited by an angel or expecting the imminent visit of one again. Finally, I can't forget that this is the land of artists, but not only Italian artists; all the Romantics dreamed of Italy. There is Liszt of course, but also Brahms or Schumann who went to the Lake Como region. I told myself that by following in their footsteps these landscapes would teach me about them and about what they had loved. You see, we keep coming back to this play of correspondences between the soul and nature. I would add that these musicians allowed me to confirm a childhood intuition: landscapes are essentially musical. The mountain I looked at as a child, hoping to meet God there, is Johann Sebastian Bach. The higher you climb, the less you see what's below and the more apt the heights become for finding yourself. The sea foreshadowed the works of Debussy, Ravel, and Janáček. Water and music share the common notion of waves, uninterrupted abundance, and the feeling that both can quench and slake our thirst. And like water, the life of the performer ebbs and flows, not only in tone but also in power and energy.

---

*St. Angelo Bridge.

†Neighborhood in Italy.

Highly gifted children are less rare than it might appear. It's often a matter of circumstance. What would we know of Mozart—who at the age of seven was giving recitals of his own compositions all over Europe—if his father, who was also a musician, had not encouraged him? The same is true of Picasso, a genius painter from the age of twelve, no doubt trained by the example of his father, a drawing teacher. Just what Yehudi Menuhin needed to prove himself right: "There are no child prodigies, only children born of parent prodigies." Tell us about your parents.

My mother was a native of Corsica and Italy. She kept its sun and solemnity. She's a woman who's always been sublime, thanks to her tempered strength of character, which I love so much. I recently read these lines by the writer Angelo Rinaldi, which really sum up the essential Corsican spirit:

> When the Italian Consulate in Bastia housed even more spies than the Russian embassy today, we had for example the appearance of an emaciated Christ figure in the nimbus of the martyrdom of Fred Scamaroni. He was a Maquis* leader who fought against the occupation armies. Betrayed by an informer, he was arrested at the end of a mountain path lined with asphodels, the flowers of lies in plant symbolism. Carted off to a prison in Ajaccio by Il Duce's Black Shirts, the Corsican Jean Moulin, anticipating the doubling of his torture, slit his wrists. With his blood he wrote on the walls of his cell: "Long live de Gaulle, Long live France."

*Rural guerrilla bands of French and Belgian Resistance fighters during World War II.

My father, on the other hand, was a teacher of Italian of great generosity and integrity. He was also from the Mediterranean. By the way, I've noticed that everyone from here are like Ulysses, making his way through the most contrary currents to escape the dangers that keep taking on new life. Because, as Salah Stétié writes as someone also warned of what's at stake, "I am a child of the Mediterranean. But my Mediterranean is the *black* Mediterranean; that of Antigone and Ulysses." My parents probably inherited this common legacy but between sun and darkness, they chose to remain solar.

When asked about your last extravagance, you replied: "Turning down an important interview so I could enjoy two hours of my mother's company." Do you feel that close to your parents?

I want to live up to what I know about my mother and what I love her for. My mother gave me her passion for life. With that passion, you can get through anything, and even better, you can preserve the integrity of your being. My father is a reserved and sensitive man. In many ways, I'm like him too: he was generous enough to let me be myself. In general, I owe my parents for carrying me with their unconditional love. If you don't have that trust in yourself, given over and over again, you have to work twice as hard. How many times have I heard this or that person tell me that he or she lacks that all-important trust? And yet, if there's one connection that matters, it's this one: the gift of life, but life given *with love.* A love that proves itself, that repeats itself, that doesn't wither, that gives again and again; a love that endures in spite of everything, because that is the meaning of education: to be able to see beyond what's happening and what needs to happen in time, and to stretch the arc between these two points that are so far apart. I never felt unwanted, or shut out of conversations. I had to listen if I wanted to grow up, and I grew up by listening carefully: I paid attention to what my parents did, just as they never failed to wrap me in their affection.

This sounds too good to be true.

Don't be so sure. I was an exhausting child, always asking questions. I couldn't stand still. I felt a constant need to exert myself, both physically and mentally, not to mention intellectually. Was I hyperactive? No doubt. Even if we have to agree on what the word means. I had no trouble concentrating. It wasn't that I was bouncing from one thing to another and getting bored with it—quite the opposite. I was capable of sustained, demanding, and exhausting concentration. I always wanted to know more, nothing could satisfy me, so much so that I imagined an unlikely solution behind everything, which I had to verify, and for which I was capable of pestering my teachers. My parents were the most considerate people I've ever known: they were always there for me, always helpful. They still are, by the way, and this lively dialogue with them is something I can't live without. A friend said that the most essential words of life are: "Please, excuse me, thank you, I love you." These words don't just describe an ideal, but are what I feel when I think of my parents.

What you remember about them is an experience of freedom. But in what sense?

I liked the fact that my parents lived their own lives. They never lived through me. And now less than ever. It's true that I'm an adult now. But that could have been devastating when I was a student. How many times did I see children at the Conservatory whose shoulders were slumped under the weight of success, because their parents found a way to take revenge on their lives through them. My parents encouraged me but never forced me to do anything. They felt that success was not measured by the fact of success and that success contained the risk of failure. They simply wanted me to be happy and in love with what I was doing, in complete freedom and by choice. At the same time, I saw classmates who were disgusted or broken by their parents' ambition, parents who clearly didn't really know their own children, who they exhausted with excessive discipline or work. My parents didn't identify with me; on the contrary, they wanted me to grow into the person that I was inside and who they had prepared me to be: a sovereign being in her "free freedom," to quote an amazing expression of Rimbaud, who clearly says that even liberty has to be liberated. How could I not thank them? From the moment I was accepted at the Paris Conservatory at the age of thirteen, they let me leave Aix-en-Provence with great confidence. I lived with host families and made regular trips home and back to Paris. Others would have been worried or demanded that I come back, or would have wanted someone to watch me. Nothing like that ever happened.

Who decided that you should take up piano? You or your parents? Do you see any connection between the world of music and that of childhood, a time when the order of things has not yet been replaced by abstract notions? This is why children can

be prodigies at a very young age, like your friend Evgeny Kissin, while the case of Rimbaud is more unusual.

I have a dual personality, easily besieged by doubt with mysterious obsessions and behaviors that could, from time to time, make me my worst enemy. This was certainly a concern for my parents, who wanted the best for me. In addition, I had a vital need to exert myself. So they looked for activities, all kinds of activities, to channel this overflow of energy. First judo, then dancing and tennis. But I remained insatiable, and none of these disciplines brought me the balance and calm I was looking for. None of them satisfied the kind of longing I had for something I could really sink my teeth into and finally find balance. This shows that this energy was more mental than physical. And suddenly music appeared. I had no contact with classical music except for the tunes my mother sang. That was until the day when I was enrolled in a music class for very young children. My classmates were all three and four years old, and I was seven. I will remember that day for the rest of my life. I felt that my life had suddenly taken a dramatic turn. Obviously I knew nothing about the future when I was seven, but at that moment, I knew there would be a before and an after. I realized that music would be a part of my life forever. It was what I'd been waiting for and what I needed. It was sealed. An hour later, when my father came to pick me up, the young woman who taught the class, Françoise Tarit, took him aside and said: "You know, I think your daughter has a talent for music. It would be a good idea for her to take piano lessons, at least to start." "Of course," my father replied. "Let's try." After that, music was my salvation. There was almost no longer any room for anything else. I say "almost" because I continued to feel the same emotional thrill I got from the horses in the Camargue. I was frustrated that I couldn't live with them permanently, just like I couldn't have a pet, even if I had accepted my parents's arguments, that they would only be unhappy in an apartment. I am still convinced that this frustration gave me the drive and energy to create the Wolf Conservation Center.

You spontaneously chose the piano. Weren't you attracted or seduced by any other instrument?

I chose music and it introduced itself to me by way of a piano. It was the only instrument in the big room where my father had taken me. Françoise Tarit asked me to sit down. She began to play the piano. She played a short piece by Schumann, which enchanted me, as I told you earlier. I remember taking longer and deeper breaths, and feeling that a way was opening. Each note released in me those "millions of keys of tenderness, of passion, of courage, of serenity," of which Proust speaks. I remained faithful to the instrument that gave me this feeling of liberation. But I could have easily become a cellist. From the first, I took a carnal, sensual approach to my instrument. One day, I was able to embrace a cello. I did this after seeing a young girl at the Conservatory playing with her eyes half-closed in concentration. Her forehead rested on the sound-post. Her slender wrist swayed nimbly with each movement of the bow. Her fingers formed arabesques on the strings. I felt such a strong intimacy between her and her instrument that I, too, felt carried away. With her, the physical embrace was total and the contact almost fatal. No cause for surprise there, I experience music through my whole body, like an experience of visitation. But in the end I decided to stay with the piano. My attraction to the cello has never faded, and the memory of that first encounter drives me to play more often with cellists than violinists. I discovered it again, intact, when I met Sol Gabetta at a chamber music festival in Germany in 2010. We each presented our own program. Several weeks later, we met again in Gstaad. We had some time to talk. I was moved by her unique approach to music—spontaneous and lively. She could have been that little girl I had glimpsed at the Conservatory years before. It was love at first sight, both musically and in terms of friendship. This meeting was all the sweeter because it was unexpected. The complicity was so obvious that we decided to extend these musical moments and record the program. The piano-cello duo works like a charm. A simple and intense understanding. Sol Gabetta reveals what moves me so strongly about this instrument—a sound that comes close to the human voice. Together we have created a dialogue between Schumann and Brahms.

Until recently, the theme park for gifted children was a boys-only affair. Your example alone disproves that predominance. An example reinforced by an actress like Jodie Foster, a gymnast like Nadia Comăneci, or a violinist like Hilary Hahn. But beware: child genius is often closer to frozen perfection than to true creativity. Arthur Rimbaud, a super thug, but a real egghead, who imitated Virgil in Latin at the age of ten, began old while Titian, who turned painting upside down at the age of ninety, ended young. André Breton spoke of the eternal genius of youth; we can therefore also speak of the ageless genius of youth. It's also amazing to see the children who are able to memorize the Torah or the Koran, and their thousands of interpretations, chess players like Étienne Bacrot, artists like Masaccio, Leonardo, Liszt . . . the list is long of great creators who were geniuses from the beginning. But it cannot hide the list of other children who despite their predispositions gave nothing and especially the list of those who waited until old age to offer, on the threshold of death, the full extent of their genius. What is it like to be a prodigy?

Children are like wax. You can make anything you want out of them. Statistically there are more chances of finding child prodigies than adult prodigies. All the difficulty lies in development. The great challenge is not childhood but adulthood. As for me, I wasn't a child prodigy. I started playing piano quite late. Let's just say that I had talent. But since then, so much work! Whether we like it or not, it all comes down to work! By that I mean work on myself, of course. But it's work that I completely accepted as a child. I didn't see it as work. I was compulsive by nature and I always wanted to work harder, to go faster, to master the technique so that I could work my way into larger repertoires. I didn't realize that few of the kids around me felt the same compulsion to overachieve. A child is never aware of the world, he *is* the world. I realized later that all the effort of studying is to return to this state, enriched by all that has been discovered in the meantime.

If music has saved you, what has it saved you from?

From myself when I felt lost as a child. I'd say it was more a case of me being isolated within myself. I had a lot of trouble getting along with kids my age. I can't say exactly why, if it wasn't because of the particular character I've just described and my disgust for the kind of cruelty that children displayed at school, which greatly disturbed me. So I withdrew into an imaginary world that I constructed to satisfy what I would call the needs of my soul. Stories, escapes, even obsessions. I was determined to make the world conform to a personal scheme that seemed ideal to me. Music saved me, and saves me every morning because it builds a bridge between the real world and my inner world. It responded to my need for beauty, which is not aesthetic but athletic: the ability, thanks to wonder, to endure the struggle to be yourself in the night of every kind of violence. Beauty is the standard that allows us to measure what is purely human, while everything is being done to dehumanize our relationship with the world, the cosmos, and the other.

When music entered my life, it opened a space of fruitful exchange for me, especially on issues that at first glance go beyond what is usually considered to be its domain. Questions about faith and death, and about the nature of my participation in the world. When I speak of music, I include all that it touches—composers, performers, and of course audiences. My meeting with Brahms was crucial. But my encounter with some of his interpreters was equally crucial. In the way they play, there's the way music saved them, and continues to save them. Music taught me how to free myself from worries and anxieties and to reinvent myself, just as the music of Bach did for Glenn Gould. Bach's music gave birth to him on earth like Gould raised him to heaven. Or Hilary Hahn in the Partitas—one chord from the musician and the universe is saved: I save myself in it by becoming music myself.

Since I was ten years old, music has never stopped defying me or fulfilling me. It either reduces me to nothing or throws me back before myself by its very presence. Like the beings that manifest the sacred essence of nature around us, I sense in advance that it will discourage my efforts to learn it, either in terms of being or in terms of things. In the same way, there's nothing to say about the standing stone on the edge of the hill or the wolf lying next to me, except that they bear witness to a friendly and overwhelming darkness in the midst of light. But as soon as I learned about the precise limits from which to approach the musical phenomenon, limits that denote a stay without limits, I realized that music, if it tends to reach its essence, if it wants to unfold from within its mystery, which remains a grace whatever the effort, can't be a pastime or a game for me.

How could it be? In a subtle dialectic, it refocuses the time that it uncovers with its veil. Despite appearances, it doesn't try to be a distraction: it brings me back to the heart of the question of all questions—that of the world, its future, and therefore mine. As I have heard it and continue to hear it, following in the footsteps of my favorite composers, music does not propose to distract man from his destiny, nor to deceive him, nor to promise him a false freedom that would chain him either to a lure or to a lie. In truth, what music has offered me, and what it has saved me to do, is to delve deeper into the mystery of existence, and the mystery of myself.

4

MUSIC WILL SAVE THE WORLD

For two years, the planet was put on hold because of the COVID crisis. You didn't play much, if at all, during this time. Then war broke out again in Europe. What do you think about this?

The pandemic we recently lived through was unprecedented. It's hard to talk about it briefly and impartially. My admiration went to the entire medical profession, which saved so many lives by working tirelessly under extreme conditions. I felt deep compassion for those who were isolated, for those who were severely infected, for those whose emergency operations had to be postponed for lack of beds, and for all the families who were plunged into mourning without being able to accompany their loved ones. When I think of the composers I love most, how can I not remember what they went through? Bach lived during the Silesian Wars, Mozart was alive at the beginning of the French Revolution, Beethoven faced the Napoleonic conquests, Brahms had to overcome the war between Austria and Prussia,

Rachmaninoff went into exile, and Shostakovich expressed the horror of the siege of Leningrad. All these great composers were not absent from their times, which were often far more violent than our own. But they all knew how to deal with it: With great humanity. What we hear in their music is the fragile harmony between the tragedy common to all people and all times and that which comes to save it, that which offers liberation. It is possible that our time once again needs a "more intense music," to use Rimbaud's expression, a music that outlines a space for living in truth, a time for loving beyond the present misery. At a time when the gloomiest predictions besiege us, in a sometimes dubious one-upmanship, let's also be very confident in the resources of harmony: it always transcends misfortune, it responds to it on a higher degree. Music is an opening to the infinite. Nothing can silence this song to come. Let's keep our ears open to what is to come, perhaps on the legs of a dove.

Don't you feel that classical music has gone out of fashion? That it is no longer audible in a world dominated by technology and material obsession? A world in which, on the one hand, we are promised the conquest of space and the systems beyond our solar system, and, on the other hand, we see unprecedented pollution, the decline of all species and our deteriorating relationship with the ecosystems, something that threatens our very future.

Not at all! Quite the contrary! In comparison to pop, to rock, to techno, classical music has its own space, but not on the same scale, whether we deplore it or not. Compared to the era of Bach, Haydn, or Mozart, the audience for classical music is considerably larger. When Bach published *The Musical Offering* at his own expense, he printed a hundred copies. Not to mention his works that were not played or rarely in his lifetime, while the *Goldberg Variations* recorded by Glenn Gould sold millions of copies. With a certain art of provocation, Gustav Leonhardt was also capable of being annoyed by Bach's success, which seemed to him to be in inverse proportion to the public's reception of his most profound message, especially in concert, during the great Passions.* After all, classical music has the clarity of the coming day, the power of the obvious. The emotions that men like Schumann, Rachmaninoff, or Silvestrov have brought to light are ageless: they are of all times and concern every generation. Simply because joy, dream, tenderness, meditation, and the expression of the inner life cannot be altered to harmonize with one era or another. Unless, of course, these ideas are themselves obsolete, in which case neither you nor I have anything left to do on this earth. But I'd like to go further. Perhaps it required the dramatic atmosphere of our times to bring out the essential appeal of classical music. For as catastrophe engulfs the earth, its cities, and its people in an unprecedented race to destruction, classical music is called upon to reveal the true use of harmony. It allows us to resist the chaos around us. It allows us to rediscover the beauty that is possible, made up of sounds never heard before. To tell the truth, I once raised a glass to the death of classical music. I still persist, in a specific sense. We have no use for old music, preserved in formaldehyde, like those animal species we keep as specimens. I like music that beats, as we say of rain.

*Bach's obituary states that he wrote five Passions, the first four of which are St. John Passion, St. Matthew Passion, St. Luke Passion and St. Mark Passion. The title of the fifth Passion is not clear.

The kind that comes from deep inside. With that je ne sais quoi of mystery mixed with light. You want examples? What pianists like Lili Kraus or Emil Gilels, and closer to our time, Maurizio Pollini or Arcadi Volodos—not to mention those who have left us like Marcelle Meyer, Radu Lupu, or Nelson Freire—did with so-called classical music, was to reinvent it, while drawing from its source with an energy that makes it contemporary. The notes are never seen as a mirror reflecting an image of the music, but as the very object of the vision, making it clairvoyant.

From Pythagoras to Pérotin, the same approach to music in its ascending and evolving form has left its stamp on generations; the desire to express silence through notes, to sing to the divinity, to commune with it through a knowledge that has never ceased to grow thanks to the value and power of numbers. These questions take us back to the mysteries of theology: How can we be one and all? How can we be one and many? How to express the fixed in movement? Or how to contain the infinite in a form? What's so special about music is that it appeals to the senses, but it appeals just as much to the soul. Have you ever asked yourself why music has existed?

That's a question I never put in those words because, since my earliest musical experience—I use this word in the sense that we talk of a sexual experience—I got my answer in how much I wanted to live and relive this moment of ecstasy—infinitely. I told you about my discovery at the teacher's thanks to Schumann.* You don't ask questions when you are convinced

*The professor from Leçons Particulières (*Private Lessons*).

you have the answer and doubt doesn't cross your mind. But we have to make a point of verifying, of putting to the test the truths on which we base our lives, if only to firm up our choices and our vocations. So yes, why does music exist? The little girl I mentioned in the preface to these conversations asked me pretty much the same thing at the end of a concert. "Music, what's the point?" Why would it exist, if not to help the most unfortunate, to save someone in the worst circumstance, to restore the heart to those who have lost it. Every performer understands very early on that it's not the musician that matters, nor the music either. It's the listener alone, and this unexpected and impossible star that rises in the sky of his sorrow, the heat in his cold, the unknown hope in the known and tormented ocean of despair. For this music is essential, and has been since the dawn of time. When it is deployed, love comes with it. It is neither in the giver nor the receiver, nor between them both. It is the exchange of one to the other. Music is this exchange; the musician is the one that inaugurates it. Shakespeare made this notion his own in *The Tempest,* his final masterpiece, when Prospero, the mage of a thousand spells, bids the world farewell so that he may be reborn to himself on another plane—finally free. Prospero then embodies the hope of love to come: He makes everyone aware of an ardent but detached serenity that survives, without erasing the sadness of tragedy that is at the heart of all existence. Why invoke Shakespeare when you ask me about the meaning of music? Because it is impossible not to make the connection between this play and Beethoven's sonata of the same name, so essential is the link between this work and the other, so much so that the composer himself emphasized it: the tempest is the time of passion. It is a heroic and contemplative passion that has found its end in a perfect revelation of the heart. At a certain height, the heart cannot be separated from the spirit that reveals it. When the feeling of love becomes so strong that it explodes from within, no word expresses it better than music. Who can deny the spiritual ecstasy into which it plunges us? The feeling it awakens and reveals in each of us, that there is nothing more wondrous, mysterious, and irreplaceable in our lives than our sentimental essence. Music illuminates the path to fulfillment that we all dream of taking and follow throughout our lives. Each piece of music tells not its own story, but ours. Each piece corresponds to a piece of creative memory. Novalis said it beautifully, "We dream of traveling through the universe—but is not the universe within ourselves? The depths of the spirit are unknown to us—the mysterious path leads inward." And Hölderlin, "Everything is rhythm, the entire destiny of man is one heavenly rhythm." In fact, music can only be understood in the moment. And the experience it offers is precisely to grasp in the moment boundlessness, fullness, and the infinite wave of unheard-of riches. The philosophers give a name to this fabled world that music offers humanity, it's the universe of infinite possibilities, a universe where everything is possible at any moment. Couldn't as much be said about love?

A music scholar like Jacques Viret takes literally the challenge posed by Orpheus, the rhapsodist of Magna Graecia: how to sing, how to bring song to the fore when death comes and tears you away from love, how to make death heard in song, that is, how to confront death and life, and make death the condition of new life? And you, Hélène Grimaud, how do you make your entirely verbal analysis audible in the music you perform?

And, first of all, what distinguishes an interpreter from a simple pianist?

Virtuosity. Virtuosity has nothing to do with performance, demonstration, or display, but indicates the highest degree of professional excellence—in all fields, incidentally, not just music. It involves skillful technique, not to be confused with dexterity. It's not just a matter of muscular control or speed. Virtuosity, and the technique it requires, should be understood as the art of finding the perfect balance, the ideal balance between what the performer wishes to be heard and what the work demands be made audible. Bach demands this virtuosity. To play him involves all the technique demanded by the work, without ever allowing this high degree of technique and speed to empty the music of its spiritual essence, or to diminish it. It means playing in such a way that one no longer knows where one begins and the other ends. It means translating this sublime alloy, the transcendence and universality of this music, I would say its mystery: the mystery that lies in everything Bach touches in the soul of everyone, at every time and in every place, even if that individual has no contact with classical music. It is therefore not by chance that composers of every era have turned to him to discover and know themselves. Beethoven, Mendelssohn, Schumann, and Brahms were deeply influenced by the choral construction of his melodies. The same is true of performers, who measure their technical and spiritual progress by playing Bach. He is a touchstone for a pianist guaranteeing the honesty of his playing.

You also asked me how I make my analysis—entirely verbal—audible in the music that I perform. I would answer without any hesitation: in the work of designing a record.

Until recently, we were content to record this or that work by a musician, or even to make a complete recording of his or her works. Today, performers don't think in terms of "concepts" but of alloys, juxtapositions, series of selected pieces to illuminate a particular vision of a state of mind or a perspective on the world. This is a more impressionistic approach but perhaps also a more philosophical one. It has the advantage of emphasizing the performer's own reflections on the very essence of music and the world, thus offering the public broader access to what is widely known as classical music. This idea is nothing new. Marcel Proust anticipated it in what he wrote about Swann's* ideas on music. His character praised the talent—among them the imaginary Vinteuil—of several great musicians "who do us the service, when they awaken in us the emotion corresponding to the theme they have discovered, of showing us what richness, what variety lies hidden, unknown to us, in that vase, unfathomed and forbidding night of our soul which we take to be an impenetrable void."

For me, it's also a reminder of why music exists, a reason that is found in Prospero's will:

And my ending is despair,
Unless I be relieved by prayer,
Which pierces so that it assaults
Mercy itself, and frees all faults.
As you from crimes would pardoned be,
Let your indulgence set me free.

*The central character in Marcel Proust's *Swann's Way*.

Which I used for example to combine *The Tempest* with Beethoven's *Choral Fantasy* and Arvo Pärt's *Credo.*

In your opinion, what does it mean to have a sense of eternity? Is this the distinguishing characteristic of musical revelation? Unless it's no more than an illusion? Of course we can create the appearance of harmony, but doesn't this pose a great risk of being deceived by them? And therefore, should we not fight against this myth superimposed on the real, as Leo Tolstoy may have thought when he created *The Kreutzer Sonata*?

To have a sense of eternity is not to place the eternal above the world, it's to be born into another reality, set within the first one, to another state of love that replaces the first in a conversion to joy. Shakespeare, for example, extends his hand to Beethoven, who passes it on to Corigliano while Pärt gives life to a Bach prelude, all united in the same fervor. The question of music may have found its answer, not in regretting the past but in creating the future.

Let me insist: What does it mean to be a classical musician today? This "fine today" in which we are told that there is no longer any theological, or even logical, guarantee.

An era is judged by what it fears and what music transcends by provoking it. The fear of hell is explained by the Gregorian chant, the long-awaited eclipse of God by the enthusiastic birth of opera, the Romantic emergence of the ego and its double, native solitude, in all symphonic music. There is a correspondence between the spiritual ascent of the artist and the drama of humanity crushed by the press of misfortune: God dead, poetry liquidated, literature exhausted, is only music left to sing in the distress of the times? To abolish all the trinkets of sonic meaninglessness: political slogans, words of disillusionment, speeches of denial. To authorize an act of faith, even in the face of doubt. And who knows, beyond death.

It's already been proven that music breaks down all ambitions, values and censorship. Maria Yudina, Sviatoslav Richter, Heinrich Neuhaus, Maria Grinberg, Viktoria Postnikova, Elisso Virsaladze; even shackled, these pianists demonstrated a freedom at work that no free country could have suspected. Something entirely given, entirely free, a je ne sais quoi ahead of itself that is perfectly arbitrary and perfectly imperative. A *reassured* openness. I am convinced that the terrible storms that threaten us, the dramatic atmosphere oppressing us, will make the urgent, vital need we have for music, or harmony, even more obvious. All forms of earthly evil, the servitude, cowardice, and lies, are, would be, will be unbearable without music, and the idea that it exists, that it can still be played and heard—it and its silence that can be called heavenly.

We are familiar with Albert Camus's observation about the singer Casella in Canto II of the *Purgatorio*: "Music creates life. It also creates death." Just think about that admirable passage from the *The Divine Comedy*, in which Dante, who has gone down into hell, meets a famous singer of his time. He asks him to sing. As he sings, the shades come to a halt, entranced, forgetting where they are, where we must *lasciare ogni speranza*.* And they

*Abandon all hope.

remain there until their merciless guards come to fetch them. You just mentioned faith and death, and you seem to combine them. Were both or either one sources of anxiety for you, and are they still?

Faith, like music, saves. Like music, faith is an antidote to anxiety. Faith is what joins people together. The content of that faith hardly matters to me. I only like the illumination it carries—it is universal, in all places and all times. At the opposite extreme, there is hardly anything but death that unites individuals to this extent. Death is the secret that joins the mother to her child, the lover with his or her beloved, and each of us to the world, beings, and things. If you love a person, the knowledge that you may lose them can only strengthen the love you bear for them. This, by the way, is largely what led me to perform what I've called "Masses for the Dead for the People who Loved Them," of Chopin and Rachmaninoff.

Don't be fooled. My approach is not morbid. It is even less detached from our time. Never before has death been so present, or perhaps so devoid of meaning. Look at the pandemic that threw the whole world into a state of mourning. Each of us was struck by the magnitude of the catastrophe. This plague carried off hundreds of thousands of people. Why? What could this mean? These are all questions we face on a daily basis, but also on a global scale, in a world plagued by madness and the war of all against all, and—this is the novelty of our century—by man's war against nature and against his own universe. The main problem is that television, among other media, can give the illusion that death is an illusion, that advertising is a remedy for our anxieties. Then, all of a sudden, someone close to you dies, or a tidal wave or a tornado wipes out innocent lives as we saw a few years ago, or else an unknown virus decimates entire cities. It doesn't bring us back to reality as we never really forgot it, but to the truth: we are mortal and we don't want to face this condition any longer.

Fragility is inscribed within each one of us. So, there is nothing incongruous about performing Chopin's *Funeral March* or Rachmaninoff's Second Sonata. By bringing their music back into our world it's an indication of a *possible* transcendence. And if music demands the same approach as God or death, it's no coincidence. This approach is situated on a line where all the points, though distinct, are connected by a thin but powerful thread, making music the preeminent meditation on God; through it, we experience death, but the order I have indicated can be reversed at will, according to a quasi-religious equivalence: God is a musical meditation, and only death can open up within us the region in which music can unfold in truth—this death we experience at each moment including in our erotic relationship with another. I have no doubts that these terms can be put together; I'm even convinced that some people can make the most of them, but without ever taking the risk of verifying the validity of these very precarious approaches in a concert.

I told you earlier that music to some extent saved me from being locked in myself. And it continues to do so, because it opens me up to the world, to those around me who are living through this era at the same time as I am, with me. I was actually able to measure this with Rachmaninoff's Second Sonata. I immersed myself in this work when I was fifteen. At that time, I tried to project my whole life into the piece. Today, it's not just my life that's important to me, but the life of the world, of the universe. An ever more beautiful and stunning universe, which I feel is radically threatened. This gives me an intense, sharp, and permanent pain, that forces me to make even more music.

The poet Philippe Jaccottet once spoke of music in these terms: "We could say that if there were no God, or gods, and that there never had been any, music like this should give birth to them . . . She seems to summon them back in this music, and they responded." Have you ever felt that way? Does this faith you are evoking have a specific name? Is it a specific religion?

It reflects a belief. I prefer to remain humble. I can't imagine having the intelligence capable of grasping the essence and form of this belief in its totality. I can't say exactly whether it's a belief in God or something else, nor can I formulate a definition of God. I believe in the sacred, and I can find it expressed in a tree, a work of art, or a church. However, there are elements of belief that I have made my own. So I believe in a world beyond this one. I think we have the power to connect with a higher, spiritual world that reflects a reality that is beyond our comprehension. Music allows us to catch a glimpse of it and, in the best-case scenario, touch it with our souls. It is pure transcendence and brings man back into his most noble humanity. It responds to fear of the future by overcoming death. It soothes. And transfigures the world below. Because we have to live! Here, now, right now. Because we don't have a spare life, so every moment must count. To be lived to the full, in exchange with others. To look them straight in the eye with a smile. That is really why empathy and compassion remain one of life's most beautiful quests, the path of which music allows us to glimpse. Firstly, because it facilitates the creation of a bond with others, with an obviousness rarely matched by any other medium. Is it the ferryman from one world to another found in so many mythologies? The anti-ferryman? You know, the character who steers the boat across the River Styx, from the shores of life to the shores of the underworld. It's the reverse journey to which music invites us—from the shores of Hell to the shores of Eden.

In addition to the best thinkers and writers who have written about music, from Vladimir Jankélévitch to Pascal Quignard, from Charles Rosen to Claude Lévi-Strauss, you told me that you read the essays of George Steiner, because, and I quote, "in them he develops an intense chain of thought on the question of the relationship between culture and barbarism."

Yes. It's a chain of thought that fuels my own on the question of music. He asks, "Does an artist bear responsibility for the dishonest uses of his inventions by barbarians?" Lukacs held Wagner as responsible to the end of time for how the Nazis used his music. In his view, faith in the resources of the future as defined by the Enlightenment is forbidden to us, and the death camps mark the boundary of the West. But Steiner is also a profound thinker about musical phenomena which he defines as the ultimate mystery of being. In the style of a postmodern Nietzsche he admits: "A life deprived of music would be a life of inconsolable sorrow." It's in this general perspective that we should understand his constant references to Mozart, whom he nicknames *alter deus* or "tutelary presence." Overall, George Steiner has made some dazzling observations about music that I love, like "Music 'keeps time' for itself and us. It adjusts the chronometer as it pleases." Or this, "It is possible that a Plato, a Carl Friedrich Gauss, a Mozart, redeem man's existence."

Do you think that music can be of any help in what you call the novelty of our time, "man's war against his own universe"?

Yes, if it isn't "the" indispensable antidote to the deafness that strikes people as soon as they are told of the impending global catastrophe threatening the planet. It even holds an unbeatable position in the awakening of consciousness. During a recent tour, I was stuck in a monstrous traffic jam caused by construction. They were building an overpass to relieve congestion at the intersection where the taxi taking me from the airport to the hotel was stuck. I rolled down the window and a kind of dreadful roar invaded the vehicle. To my left was a giant bulldozer. Jackhammers were everywhere. Concrete cylinders were being rolled into place. And above this cacophony, the honking of irate motorists. All of a sudden, I imagined that I had the power to mute this sound and broadcast Johann Sebastian Bach's "Siciliano"* to this metropolis and to this very spot. This music would undoubtedly give its listeners a salutary jolt. It would undoubtedly make them hear the ineptitude of our way of life and the horror of what we impose on ourselves. It's an experience I dream of having every time I find myself in a similar situation. What other verb speaks to humanity universally of beauty and harmony, and at the same time manages to awaken in us, in the depths of our time, a nostalgia for Eden? Who could forget

*Reference to the Siciliano movement from Bach's Flute Sonata No. 2.

that in the Kingdom of the Spirit, all angels are musicians? Who could do without them? On the other hand, the question arises every day: In whose interest is this murdered? What is served by making us deaf and blind? I have my own ideas on this: those who refuse their "fatality for happiness," as Rimbaud said. What could give greater pleasure than to have rapport with Bach, Beethoven, and Brahms? I could add Debussy, Ravel, and Alban Berg to this list, and if you want more, it could be a child's laughter. By liberating us, it restores our original freedom without which nothing, no vocation, no destiny can be lived. So, how can we be free if in a world in its death throes we are deaf to Bach, Beethoven, and Brahms? What vocation can be sustained if no one hears the call or is able to spread it?

To paraphrase a famous phrase coined by Dostoevsky for Prince Myshkin, do you think music could save humanity, as you say it saved you?

I'm sure it could, provided we let everyone hear it, and what could be easier than a universal language? Music is the art of reconciliation. More than ever, I agree with André Breton when he said, following the thought of Novalis: "Everything tends to make us believe that there exists a certain point in the mind where life and death, the real and the imaginary, the past and the future, the communicable and the incommunicable, the high and the low cease to be perceived as contradictions." In my opinion, it is this point in the mind that music touches and reveals. All the forces of life collide in music, which reconciles them. Love and hate are overcome. Music is life's triumph over our natural tendency to destroy. Music is also the experience of silence. So finally, what is a musician good for if he has to be good for something? You see, we continue to circle around this question. Well, I think it is the great consoler—and who would deny that our need for consolation is insatiable, as the Swedish writer Stig Dagerman has noted? The musician consoles us by reminding us of beauty, and by giving it life and language. I don't know if music is enough to justify our presence on Earth, but it redeems the horrors of which we are capable. It is a form of charity, perhaps its tonal key. When I listen to music, I often think of the philosopher Simone Weil's heartbreaking observation a few months before her death, when she confessed her powerlessness to reconcile these two extremes: God's greatness and extreme human misery. Music offers this reconciliation. It offers man this opening to beauty and the way to approach it. It shows him that here is something else besides these conflicts, dramas, and difficulties that humanity goes through, and which every individual experiences in a difficult situation as a pain that often cannot be communicated. Hence this feeling of loneliness that we all experience at one time or another—whether it's our own or something we see in another person. It's true that music doesn't solve anything, but I'll say it again, what a consolation! It teaches us, as Rimbaud demanded, to celebrate life rather than cursing it. For the rest of my life I will remember with all my body and soul the day when I knew not only that I would devote my life to it as my first teacher, Françoise Tarit did, but that it would be a balm, a path, and a resource for my whole life. I was ten or eleven years old. I had barely begun to study the piano; I had heard Alban Berg's *Piano Sonata*. I was—how can I put it—fascinated by it, in the primary sense of the word. Like a mouse in front of a snake, I couldn't stop listening to it. There were colors, vibrations, and something extremely poignant. I was entering a mysterious world and at the same time wondering how music could create or even reveal that world. I asked to hear it again, and again I felt this fascination, this feeling of being brought into the world, full of both pain and promise. I thought about what it evoked in me, and it still does, so much so that I built an entire record, *Resonances*, around it. The emotions it evoked were mine alone, while at the same time I felt very close to the soul of the composer. In fact, if you play this piece well—with the utmost attention and concentration—Alban Berg's soul rises to the surface of the notes.

Would you go so far as to say that music is a form of shamanism? I know how much you love Native American culture.

How could you not love Native American culture? It is fully summed up in this saying, commonly attributed to Chief Seattle, "Treat the earth, nature, and animals as they should be; they were not given to you by your parents, they were lent to you by your children." Or in this prophecy from Sitting Bull, "Only when the last tree has been cut down, the last fish been caught, and the last stream poisoned, will they realize they cannot eat money."* And can there be any doubt that music is a form of shamanism? If music grips us so intensely, it's because it builds a bridge to the beyond, just as the shaman tried to do, who is the mediator between man and spirit—that is, the quintessence of the living, the manifestation of transcendence. It allows us to

*Although this quote is sometimes attributed to Sitting Bull, it is more widely attributed to the Cree, a Native American tribe of Canada.

go far beyond what we know and what we think we know, and especially far beyond what we are. It is the possibility of elevation through emotion and honesty: there are no fake versions. It is a question of truth, simply because music doesn't try to demonstrate anything, or prove anything. It reveals the invisible chords of the world and reconciles all opposites—just like shamanism. It is a truth that carries its own proof: it believes and compels belief in it. It opens a higher world that it lets us hear and see. It gives the world perfection and harmony. It makes us seers of the invisible. In this way, I think it is a form of spirituality. When I was sixteen, before I had encountered the Native American world and culture, I stumbled upon an intriguing theory by Isaac the Syrian that I've never forgotten. According to him, God created the angels in silence and, positioned at the boundary of the spiritual and the material, man who unites in himself all the planes of the universe by "composing the unique harmony made up of different sounds." So, in his view, the human being is a cosmic being, a musical being. And it is the pulsation of this cosmic life that explains part of his being. This sixth-century writer, mystic, ascetic, and bishop combined man, harmony, and the universe. What better way to express the spiritual essence of music?

But isn't that the very definition of art? Would music be more so than other artistic disciplines?

I prefer to avoid comparisons. They are always reductive. But music undeniably has three characteristics that are unique to it and distinguish it from the other arts. As a philosopher like Schopenhauer pointed out, it is not subject to mimesis, nor to does it have any relationship to reality. It doesn't resemble anything, nor does it give the impression of anything. It is the meaning of its meaning. Here we are in the pure realm of creation. Then, if the order of discourse in poetry is to go forward, the order of music is to go back to the beginning, to find our untouched origin and bring us back to it. Finally, music cannot exist without a performer. In this art of chords, the concord between composer and performer is fundamental if the miracle is to take place: the mystery of creation when it is at work in the deepest depths of our being. Furthermore, I define the role of performer, at least as I see it, as that of a medium—or a shaman. The shaman listens to the wind, rain, stars, and spheres, to the water and forests. I have to surrender myself entirely to the evidence of the composer in order to establish a connection between him and the listener. It's one thing to feel and understand the universe and the emotions expressed by these black notes on a staff; it's quite another to make them sound as close as possible to my own emotions and feelings. Interpreting as a performer means allowing the composer to be present in the moment of playing through the medium of my presence. And this is where the spiritual nature of this art finds its specificity, its greatness, its very honor. Music is the art of incarnation—at least for me. It brings us into the heart of this mystery and the possibly overwhelming nature of its revelatory power. Each musical work does not tell its own story but our own. Each piece corresponds to a piece of creative memory.

5

AT THE PIANO

> *He knew that the very memory of the piano falsified still further the perspective in which he saw the elements of music, that the field open to the musician is not a miserable stave of seven notes, but an immeasurable keyboard (still almost entirely unknown) on which, here and there only, separated by the thick darkness of its unexplored tracts, some few among the millions of keys of tenderness, of passion, of courage, of serenity, which compose it, each one differing from all the rest as one universe differs from another, have been discovered by a few great artists who do us the service when they awaken in us the emotion corresponding to the theme they have discovered, of showing us what richness, what variety lies hidden, unknown to us, in that vast, unfathomed and forbidding night of our soul which we take to be an impenetrable void.**

I know you like this passage in *Swann's Way* by Marcel Proust. How do you make the mystery work for you? Do you have a method?

---

*Trans. by C. K. Scott Moncrieff, Terence Kilmartin, and Andreas Mayor. Revised by D. J. Enright.

Unfortunately, no. There is no automatism. The performance of a work cannot be systematic, even if it has been worked on scrupulously. Nothing is ever given on principle. Playing is like grace or prayer. Miracles don't happen at every concert. Nor does it happen with just any composer. Every performer finds her elective affinities with several composers—echoing the harmonics of soul and sensitivity, and according to the predisposition of youth. We need to find our own "sound." This is the prerequisite for much more than a simple performance: a recreation of the work. And yet, at certain concerts, this is not possible. It's frustrating, but it's also wonderful, because playing becomes an eternal new beginning. I have to reinvent myself every time I go on stage. Moreover, this miracle doesn't just depend on me—the orchestra also plays its role—and how! There is an alchemy that takes place, a kind of "on the route" as Rimbaud understood it. A fusion that I would compare to love, when two bodies recognize each other, find each other, and become one for the time that this love exists, which in this case would be the time of the concert. The orchestra is obviously a multiple body endowed with a single head: the orchestra conductor, and the miracle doesn't happen with all of them. But when it does happen, you attain moments of pure joy. For example, I remember the recording of Rachmaninoff's Second Concerto with Vladimir Ashkenazy. We had never worked together before but even before the recording began, which took place in London, I was convinced that if I recorded this piece with him, something very special would happen. We started early in the morning, at nine o'clock. It was cold. The city was covered in fog. Everything fell into place the moment the maestro lifted his baton. If there was a shadow of a doubt about the tandem initiated by this recording, it was instantly dispelled. We hadn't even spoken together, but we recognized each other. We played the whole concerto in one go, and he followed me with the most marvelous flexibility. Of course, Vladimir Ashkenazy's particular fondness for Rachmaninoff is well known. Since his career began he has been an unwavering champion of this composer. But I've rarely experienced such clarity in working with a conductor and orchestra under his direction. I was doubly happy as this Rachmaninoff recording was challenging. My first record at the age of fifteen was dedicated to him. I grew up with his music. Paradoxically, returning to what we already know also means losing our footing. It's a good way to measure the distance you've traveled from yourself! With this second recording, I couldn't do any worse than the first, nor could I be satisfied with doing as well. It had to be better and different, without any bias toward uniqueness. This second record couldn't be a commentary on the first. I wanted it to be completely free of references to my first work. So it was maximum risk, but that's a feeling I love, the risk of pushing myself to the limit and everything hanging by a thread. That hasn't diminished as I've grown older. The secret of a true performance is to embody what you are playing at the moment *ad hoc.* The young girl I was at fifteen doesn't think like I do, although we remain very close. Similarly, I waited twelve years to record Brahms's Second Concerto, after recording his First Concerto under the direction of Kurt Sanderling. Everything clicked when I met the orchestra conductor Andris Nelsons. I knew the time had come to attack this extremely difficult and complex work that I had been content to play from time to time in concert. When the challenge is met, I know of no greater joy than that experienced in these special moments. In a concert, the audience also grasps the magic fully. It also plays a very important role in making the miracle happen, through the attention it gives during the performance—a palpable acuity that almost becomes the performer's own breath. It provides the final touch, the vibration of life that defines music as the most splendid metaphor for the world of emotions.

Have you often experienced this intense symbiosis with an orchestra? I remember rehearsals over the years whether with Kurt Sanderling, Vladimir Ashkenazy, Christoph Eschenbach, Vladimir Jurowski, David Zinman, Manfred Honeck, Valery Gregiev, or Teodor Currentzis, in which the various connections each time seemed close to a form of perfection.

I don't know what you mean by "often." It's happened—I haven't kept count—but at the peak, like this time, not so often. I remember a concert with the Bavarian Radio Chamber Orchestra. We played Mozart's Piano Concerto Nos. 19 and 23. During the performance, I felt an incredible, very special sensation as if the music had lifted me up and carried me off in a kind of flight over my instrument and the entire orchestra. I knew all the musicians quite well, but that evening, something like a miracle occurred. I experienced a moment of grace with them that I dream of finding again every time I go on stage. I also knew that I couldn't play better. The story had some unpleasant consequences. A few days later I'd been scheduled to record these concertos with Claudio Abbado in Bologna, Italy. The memory of excellence that I had kept from my experience with the Bavarian Radio Symphony Orchestra created a kind of stiffness that had a negative influence on my partnership with

Claudio. We could no longer agree on the tone to be given to the two works, especially the cadenza of the Concerto No. 23. We had endless discussions about authenticity and purity of interpretation, and I was in favor of following the example of Mozart himself, who improvised while performing his own works. The cadenza is the moment when the musicians put down their instruments to leave the floor to the soloist alone, and the choice of the cadenza, if not written by the composer, remains the prerogative of the soloist. I didn't want to give that up. I wanted to play Busoni's cadenza. I discovered it when I was thirteen when the version Horowitz recorded with the Milan Scala Orchestra conducted by Carlo Maria Giulini came out, and it blew me away. There was a tug-of-war with Claudio. In the end, that was the cadenza we played, but no doubt because of our many discussions, we didn't experience the wonderful osmosis, the blended, organic relationship that I had so often experienced with him before.

Is this the reason why, unlike Glenn Gould, who was quick to say no, you prefer concerts?

Absolutely. There is the promise of everyone at each new concert. Recording in a studio is perhaps more likely to produce a perfect result from the technical or acoustic point of view, if not from an intention point of view, because we can always go back to correct and re-record a passage, but it lacks the essential as far as I am concerned. That would be the initial impulse of the work provided by the communion with the audience. Again, music is spiritual because it connects us in a universal way, not only to this higher world, but to each other. The concert gives the work and its interpretation its full meaning: to be heard in unison. It is in the concert that we can fully speak of incarnation, and what happens is always unique and profoundly human. There's a vitality in the concert that I always strive for. The score becomes the center of the universe, and all I have to do is honor what it obliges me to do: to deliver everything it contains, everything it offers me, in one direction only: in an upward movement, to open that access to the universal that is the hallmark of music. These moments of freedom shared with the audience are extraordinary moments where nothing matters, where you take all the risks, where you question everything, where you concentrate not only on what you're playing but also on what's going on in the room, aware of being that ferryman between one world and another that I mentioned earlier. Also aware of being the lieutenant of the music. That's when the magic moment comes, when everything seems to be in perfect alignment, when you feel that everything is there, without compromise, in perfect balance. This moment only happens very rarely. And it is both sad and happy. It's happy because its rarity proves that it's not the result of a recipe or some plan learned by heart. If that were to be the case, this would no longer be an art but a craft. You must have the humility to accept it. It's hard to experience, especially if you are a perfectionist. We want it to be what we know it can be, what we know it should be! Unfortunately, we have to grieve for it. And start over again. Prepare as best you can, hoping that something will come for which the performer is not responsible. Something I call the visitation. The visitation of what or who, I don't know. Sometimes it is the composer. Sometimes it's a much more universal presence than that of the author himself. Sometimes when I play Brahms, I have had the impression he was there. Really. And I think people feel the concert much more intensely then. But sometimes, it's the feeling that it is the very essence of the music that is visiting us. "We" the performer, the orchestra, the audience.

But, recording in the studio is the ultimate expression of the work. You can be sure that you haven't missed any nuance, anything that you wanted to express, and the studio protects you from failure.

Of course. However, it's not in the pursuit of perfection, but in the pursuit of embodiment that we reach the pinnacle of sharing. It's in this sense that I understand what Yves Bonnefoy wrote, "Imperfection is the peak." It's the human part, the opposite of the mechanical, the part of the truest emotion at a given moment—why this one rather than another—that allows the miracle to take place. The concert is an invitation to a communion, a symbiosis between the work and the audience. There's also the relationship with time that interpretation always inaugurates. It implies a magnificent unity between the composer, whom it somehow resuscitates, the performer who embodies him and the listener. Everything happens in that singular instant created by the music during the concert, a time added to the ordinary time that it unstitches. Success is as fleeting as failure. And every morning, it all has to start again. Each day is a musical adventure. From one concert to the next, I continue to be surprised—if not amazed—by the evolution of my own relationship to the work. I can't stop noticing the work this work is doing within me and its reshaping of convictions I've held for a long time. The work keeps putting me back in my place, and it is the moment when I accept or allow the possibility of failure that everything becomes possible.

I've read that in the past concerts were organized in China that were reserved for a few close friends. If a European had managed to join this select audience, he would have been struck dumb with amazement: all the musicians were in place playing their instruments, but in such a way to produce no sound. The flute was right next to the lips and the drumhead adjacent to the drumstick. But all contact was carefully avoided. This didn't prevent the orchestra from indulging in the usual mimicry of other orchestras. The audience followed the pianist's casual gestures and inspired bows with rapt attention. It enjoyed the sheer pleasure of the sequence of notes it could have heard, but didn't need any more than an archaeologist needs an architect to reconstruct an ancient city (he grasped the design perfectly through the ruins). Let's say in fact that the actual execution would have been irritating. For all the physical pleasure it would have given the audience, it would have prevented the birth of a thousand intellectual pleasures; if there had been an execution, there would have been no more playing. Could you describe a perfectly successful concert?

Music is nothing if you don't feel it. You have to create it yourself. Then it has a life. Order above all. There are no random rhythms or sounds, but nothing is left to calculation. The moment determines the inspiration; no ease, no license, but an active freedom; respect for and research into the rarest and most profound matter; concern for full, taut form; the rigorous unity of a music open to infinity, wrapped in the core that hides itself;

a painting by allusion, images awakened from one another, with no visible connection other than a fleeting relationship of lines; the inner vision magnified by the moving spectacle of forms, those clouds in the wind, nature as a breviary of memories, nothing that paints or fixes. All the mind on the level of dreams. In other words, extraordinary, rare moments. And sometimes grace just doesn't show up.

How do you react to criticism, sometimes praiseworthy, sometimes virulent? I'm reminded of André Gide, who once said that his friend Jacques Copeau had given his magazine "the consecration of precious hostilities."

Criticism is always going to be virulent at some point, and you just have to accept it. You need to lend it an ear because there is often something right in what they are criticizing you for. As artists, we know better than anyone what we are capable of doing. Nor should we dwell too much on it if we find it unjustified. The performer, in embodying his function, is necessarily upstream of the listener. The full value of a performer lies in the discovery or revelation of new sound sensations that his or her playing elicits. This discovery is one that is connected to a nuance, to the very vision of an original form. The interpretation can be disconcerting and rejected, but you must take risks and accept that you won't be followed or heard, because the musical form—and this is the only such artistic form—can only be the fruit of a creation that is constantly updated in the moment it is played. It's true that the performer has the power to elevate or destroy the music. Liszt wrote: "What constitutes the beauty of the performance cannot be set down on paper." It also happens that the critic has a very definite idea of what that beauty is, and that idea doesn't coincide with yours. This is not a serious problem. It's never the critics that pose a problem for the performer, but the secret nature of the work and the strange relationship that forms between it and the person who interprets it. The work gives the command, but it's the performer who reveals and serves it. It's a terrible responsibility when you think about it, and too few people think about it.

You work in one of the most refined of disciplines and one of the most elaborate of arts because it requires the presence of an instrument, and you devote part of your life to preserving nature in its wildest expression. Isn't there a contradiction or even a paradox between the two?

There is no contradiction between nature and music. People may think so if they feel that art is a sophisticated, elitist art, because of the enormous amount of humble and repetitive work that it demands—there is no improvisation possible when you read a score!—and also because of the instrument that is necessary to play it. In fact, there is no art that is more of a "first" art. The voice of music is direct, sensual, and primal. It calls to our instincts and our inner voice. It gives us access to a certain essence of our soul: that part of ourselves that we can give to others. But to say that music is a luxury, as I've sometimes heard people say, is a terrible mistake! It's thanks to an art like music that every individual can achieve complete fulfillment as a human being. It's thanks to music that we feel alive on a level that is not at all intellectual, because it reminds us of who we are. We also experience this awareness at the heart of wild nature, as I've experienced it with my wolves. Both in different ways provide a sense of fusion between the individual and the world, and the ties that bind us to creation, because everything is connected, every intuition responds to a total intuition. Both tell us, or tell us again, that we belong together to this ceaselessly moving and transforming creation. I believe that nature is essential to music because it is the ultimate muse. Many composers wrote their masterpieces after a walk in the countryside—Schubert, Brahms, Mahler, and Debussey to name but a few. They stylized the emotions that nature whispered to them. In my recent concerts, I have recalled these connections, especially the one between water and music, through some of the compositions by Janáček, Albéniz, Debussey, and Liszt, whose symphonic poem *Orpheus* humanizes the inhuman through the harmonic and melodic grace of its song. It also shows how music transforms the human being through its absoluteness. For me nature is the very presence of the divine, the reign of the spirit, to which music brings the blessing of art.

Is there a connection between ecology and spirituality? This idea was already visible in the work of the great medieval German composer Hildegard von Bingen (1098–1179), who said that man is "the garment of God."

Absolutely! This is why I believe that ecology cannot be considered as a simple scientific discipline or a subject for experimentation—and much less the property of a political party! It is spiritual in nature because it touches the realm of the sacred, the very essence of our relationship with the living. Again, everything is connected, and everything connects us.

I really feel the need to emphasize this point: ecology is profoundly spiritual. The whole of nature is a theophany. It is our duty to not only preserve it but to honor it, if not worship it.

How can music help in education?

If I had to improvise an answer, I'd say that music, like all education, teaches us to keep in mind the essential and the only thing that matters: our access to truth and the universal by earning our status as human beings. We have so much to lose if we lose sight of that. Nature has the same power to open and uplift the mind. Both inculcate a lesson of humility and honesty. Both force us to confront an extremely formative feeling: fear, which is generally caused by the unknown. The unknown of a work or instrument. The unknown of a mountain, a forest, the behavior of a wolf or an animal. To overcome our fear, we must curb our urge to withdraw or act aggressively and tame this new element we encounter. Defeating it is a true joy. For example, look at the piano: It's the most independent of all instruments. It's the most independent instrument there is, but it's also a very intimidating one, and even though the repertoire dedicated to it is very large and you can choose the work that suits you best—the one you hear most closely—the fact remains that the performer is alone on stage with this massive instrument, which has a very organic, percussive sound, and it has to be made to sing like an orchestra. So you have to achieve this alchemy: to make the sound you hear in your head come alive in reality. In my playing, I have to give the piano more color and timbre in its sound than the whole orchestra. The pianist faces a constant challenge: he must transform his percussion into flowing chords through an exclusively vertical action. It's a constant battle—also a battle against oneself—with determined attention and a sense of danger, but one that is accepted and inevitable.

We're all familiar with Jorge Luis Borges's story, written with his consummate art of paradox, about how a writer recreates Don Quixote by copying it. But you, like all interpreters, are not an inert mirror: You have your curve, like all mirrors. And you inevitably give scores the reflection of your own being. There's a form and a possibility of salvation here, which gives rise to a wonderful hope in the power of the interpreter: We can fantasize about God in the same way—he leaves his creation to its own devices, and in the end it imposes itself on him, just as a Pablo Casals imposed himself on Bach or a Clara Haskil on Mozart. In your opinion, what is the specificity of the interpreter in relation to other artists, painters, writers, and sculptors?

He embodies the work that he plays; without this embodiment the work will not reveal itself, but there is still something else. There is an undeniable part of re-creation in his playing. This is probably what separates the musician who *interprets* a work from excellent amateurs. It's all expressed in the word. The real value of any great interpreter is to make us discover new tonal sensations in the work, to update them, to expand the harmonic formula of the work. It's an exercise, a search, an extremely difficult task, because it's only possible if one is willing to do it. But this new, revitalized interpretation, born of a sovereignly free creative impulse, pushes the limits of interpretation even further, forcing a formidable leap forward. It's a matter of being more and more ourselves without distorting the profound essence of the work, without breaking the thread that binds us to it. And the interpretation must be legitimate—by which I mean that it must give voice to this new breath, that it must actualize the work at the moment it is played. Again, the interpreter must have the gifts of a medium: nothing in music is created *ex nihilo.* There are forms, rhythms, and sonic sensations inherent in every epoch that interpretation is predestined to through a kind of intuition. Like Glenn Gould with Bach, to name but one.

In a sense, the expert interpreter is the one who perfectly illustrates the etymology of the word. Interpretation is a word that comes from the Greek *hermeneutic,* which means the science of the God Hermes.* Hermes is the brother of Apollo, the son of the she-wolf, the god of the arts. He is the god of commerce and communication, but also of thieves. He is the liaison between people. Whenever a connection is made, whatever it may be—whenever one thing is connected to another—that is the mark of Hermes, a laughing, swift, fickle god. Hermes has given us two words: hermeneutics, the art of interpretation, and hermeticism, the art of concealing meaning. From the outset, interpretation can be understood in two ways: to make clear what is obscure, or to allow entrance into the obscurity of a message that is more or less explicit or needs to be made explicit.

There are four different types of interpretation in medieval theology: Literal, Symbolic, Allegorical, and Prophetic. In Islamic theology, as it appears in Shiism, the idea of interpret-

*Also known as the science of interpretation, or the theory and methodology of interpretation, especially the interpretation of biblical texts, wisdom literature, and philosophical texts. Also known as the "science of Hermes" because Hermes—as the messenger of the gods—was the "interpreter" between mortals and the divine realm.

ing a sacred text goes even further. It's a matter of collaborating with the Koran, the meaning of which always exists only in the interpretation, which brings about an additional meaning that was not foreseen, though necessary. Applied to music, it seems that the meaning of a great interpretation is hardly certain: Is it to render what is written, to reveal it in a prophetic, (i.e. hitherto unseen) form? Or to use the text as a pretext to give birth to something else that requires all the unique genius of the interpreter?

After all, the interpreter is invested with one mission: to constantly expand the field of the music he or she plays. It's his or her responsibility to introduce people to lesser-known composers or to give contemporary composers an audience. It's a risk—not all classical audiences have this curiosity, or at least they haven't had the right education, or they've rarely had the opportunity to listen closely to what's being composed today. In my last album, *The Messenger,* I recorded the works of the Ukrainian composer Valentin Silvestrov, who sought inspiration by rummaging through the repertoire of centuries. In 1996 he wrote, and dedicated to his late wife, *The Messenger,* a work in which he freely combines various motifs borrowed from Mozart with some touches of Schubert and accents of Wagner. "My music is a response and an echo of what already exists," he once said, and his words immediately moved me for what they suggested of correspondences and bridges that span the centuries. Moreover, his work compelled me to approach composers I had not spontaneously approached in my youth, like Mozart. When I was younger, I was drawn to the rocks that create the crashing noise of the waves and their ascent as clouds of foam. Mozart's "lightness of being" seemed strangely frustrating to me. And what can we say about Silvestrov's pure means and moderate emotions, *a fortiori*! Last but not least, I liked something about Silvestrov that touches the soul very intimately, his power to evoke nature and the elements. Pieces that float like clouds. Like animals, they are what they are—inevitable, ephemeral, fleeting and constant. Immersing oneself in this music is based on the same principle as immersing oneself in nature—a timeless place elsewhere and essential chords, Silvestrov reflects shimmering rays of light from above through a veil of tender contemplation. I see the role of the interpreter as that of a mediator, a channel between the composer and the audience, a bridge between worlds: the world of today, the world of yesterday, and the world of tomorrow. The title is therefore appropriate.

You were a student of Geneviève Joy-Dutilleux, I remember sitting next to her husband, Henri Dutilleux at one of your concerts at the Théâtre des Champs-Élysées. In general, which contemporary composers have you recorded works by?

Arvo Pärt and his *Credo*. I found it very touching that he traveled to the Tate Modern in London on February 7, 2003, where I was performing with the London Sinfonietta, to listen to the premiere of his *Lamentate*, a work he composed in honor of the artist Anish Kapoor and his sculpture *Marsyas*. I have also recorded Corigliano's *Fantasia on an Ostinato,* which is on the same record as this *Credo* conducted by Esa-Pekka Salonen, who is also a composer. Esa-Pekka and I had met for dinner several months earlier to discuss the broad outlines of the recording, which we were about to make. Esa-Pekka has an amazing air of eternal youth, although he is more than that; he is a powerful man of boundless energy with true inner strength. I learned to appreciate that he possessed, even in the turn of a simple phrase, that gift that in the end one prefers over all others, to grasp the secret fiber, to bring to light the root of human feelings and desires.

Finally, I worked with other composer-conductors, like Pierre Boulez, whom I remember with awe. It was the same year as the Arvo Pärt concert, 2003. It's amazing to think that we two French people ended up playing Bartók's Third Concerto in California. It wasn't so much Boulez's intellectual power that amazed me, but his extreme gentleness, a sign that I was looking at a very accomplished man.

Pierre Boulez conducted with an air that I found, rightly or wrongly, inspiring. When he conducted, all the planes of the musical edifice rise up and buttress each other; the cathedral creates itself out of movement. In June of the same year, I played in Amsterdam under the direction of the composer Péter Eötvös. This composer has such a direct relationship, as the conductor of the work he is interpreting, that he gives the impression he is recreating the score from its very source. Finally, there was also John Adams. An electric being, with a remarkable youthfulness of spirit—another composer who conducts like no other conductor does, which has nothing to do with the quality of this or that one's performance; one feels John Adams' solidarity with each piece, as if he were personally confirming to the passing composers that the baton has indeed been passed on. In the second half of the concert, he premiered "On the Transmigration of Souls," written in memory of the victims of the September 11, 2001, attacks in New York. As fate would have it, I happened to be at the Royal Albert Hall that evening. Coincidence had caught me and we had come full circle: from screaming to silence; the in-between that only music can try to stabilize.

Are there any pianists who you admire?

I would like to think that, from Alfred Cortot to Anna Vinnitskaya, from Sviatoslav Richter to Yuja Wang via Daniil Trifonov or Beatrice Rana, there is truly only one pianist, the same but always different, who enjoys playing with the nuances of his unique, infinitely ramified talent. In this respect, I always listen to my colleagues with passion. Whoever they are, and whatever their age or rank. I like, for example, Martha Argerich, whose sensitive presence has counted for so much in my life at times when I was in doubt. I admire her at the piano for being such a saint in the order of spiritual sensuality. She lives in a never-ending ascent, but not on the moral scale: she's constantly climbing toward self-fulfillment. I could mention some other colleagues though, both past and present—Samson François, Arthur Rubenstein, Alfred Brendel, Maria João Pires—but I think it would be better to write another book on this subject, later. I would like to add one more name, Claudio Arrau, the dream model of the freest song in its most rigorous form. Such a musician can only strengthen a vocation. He doesn't close any door; he opens them all. His example does not indicate an end but a threshold. If I like him so much, it's not because he is so superior to other pianists, that's meaningless, but because he listened to a voice from far away, from even farther away, a voice of tenderness and new violence: *the voice of music itself,* a voice to which he was able to make each one of us sensitive. In his intense and poetic quest for the gravitational forces of the depths, he evokes a je ne sais quoi kind of melancholy that is more passionate than serene.

Do you like other kinds of music besides classical?

*Chanson française,** Brassens, Barbara, Ferrat. And many other things, from jazz to Radiohead, if not Eminem, who is a very good rapper. This kind of listening has enriched my perception of classical music, just as I'm sure classical music would enrich those who don't listen to it because they think they don't have the right. As for classical music, it's the Bach we find in techno bass, the Prokofiev in Sting's work, or the Chopin in Serge Gainsbourg's. I'm against all boundaries, especially when they deprive us of a pleasure we don't know. I would like classical music to be listened to without any preconceptions: Rachmaninoff again offers us a soaring flight over the world; the Beatles remembered this almost down to the last note in their psychedelic songs of Sergeant Pepper. It's necessary to invite everyone, without any age difference, to listen to everything. There is nothing worse than being locked up. I often hear it said that young people no longer have an ear for classical music, that they find it boring. When I was fifteen, I couldn't stand being told that I was too young to play Rachmaninoff, or that I should avoid Brahms's repertoire because I wasn't athletic enough. I wouldn't say today that my elders have no right to be heard because they are too old. That amounts to the same thing! What matters is not age, or even a youthful spirit, but the spirit of childhood. There are wonderful eighty-year-old children and

*French song.

prepubescent old men and women. And I am absolutely convinced that classical music is not an antique that gets dusted off from time to time in concert halls, and is only of interest to senior citizens. It saved me. Could I be so arrogant to think that only I can hear it? Can it still move young people? My answer is of course, it is ageless and timeless. I would tell young people: Take the first step.

You are also friends with Françoise Hardy.

What I love about Françoise Hardy is first of all her voice. She has a delicate voice, neither weak nor fragile. It is a voice that attracts attention and emphasizes her singularity. We sense in her a suffering that arises from a past that has been overcome—a past that instead of creating awkward heaviness inspires affection. Beautiful, whole, and unusual, I admired her from the day we met. She has an elegance that wears no mask, that rejects all pretenses, that refuses the *false* and the *simulated.* What also strikes me is that Françoise Hardy is a welcoming person—she supports young people, but she also has expectations—she wants them to live up to their aspirations for love and friendship. What better way to start a collaboration. Ours was born when we dined together one evening during the Fête de la Musique. Orchestras were playing in the streets. We laughed and asked ourselves, "Why not us?" So we recorded "La valse des regrets," which has the peculiarity of being at the point where our respective worlds intersect; a Brahms waltz transformed into a song of its own in the tradition of what Gainsbourg had already done with Brahms, the Brahms who lived the "naïve rhythms" dear to Rimbaud.

I also know that you value your friendship with certain colleagues quite highly. I am thinking, for example, of the late pianist Nicholas Angelich, who never missed one of your concerts, and with whom you enjoyed discussing Brahms.

Nicholas Angelich is a wonderful musician who is sorely missed by our world or, to put it another way, one who our cruel world doesn't realize how much he is missed. I would like to say of him, as of other friends who have died prematurely, what Jean Cocteau said: "Poets don't die. They only give way to their true selves. They are therefore as little dead as possible." I knew Nicholas Angelich at the Paris Conservatory. We used to meet after concerts or with Jacques Thelen when I was visiting France. He was a larger than life, hypersensitive individual. The mixture of the colossal and the subtle in a man like him, who was more distinguished by his humility than his pretension, never ceased to amaze. One could sense in him a dual nature and offset imbalance that gave charm to his entire being. I often think of him, just as I do of Lars Vogt, who died a few months later at the same age.

6
THE REBEL SOUL

You have spoken of your fondness for Brahms, but are there any other composers today who attract you? And why?

I come back to Schubert, who is a composer I worked with as a child and teenager under the guidance of my teacher Pierre Barbizet who always told me, “Remember, a musician is only as great as the greatness he reveals in his fellow man.” I wasn’t looking for Schubert. It was he who appeared to me, especially in his last sonatas. It would be impossible for me to tell you why he came back to me, but I do know what he allows me to express in my playing. The theme of memory and, consequently, the theme of recollection, which is the journey of memory. I have noticed that when we remember an event, such as something that happened in our childhood, we do not remember it as the first time we experienced it and made it a memory, but as it was at the last time we remembered it. I find this phenomenon of juxtaposition fascinating and I feel it very strongly in Schubert’s work. Playing and listening to Schubert makes us travelers, in the sense he gives this word in his *Winter Journey:* A pilgrim travels through heaven and hell without ever stopping. Could it also be that Schubert brings me back to nature, and a devastated creation? His work gives music an eternal background in a world that we would like to think is doomed. I find in it this magical movement of music, which is also a look into the future, but cast in the beautiful light of nostalgia, melancholy and sadness. That's what I want to make audible again: this gyration, the tempo of ecstasy, the saving impulse of contemplation through music.

To illustrate what I'm saying, I'd like to quote what Lie Tseu* writes in The True Classic of Perfect Emptiness, in which he perfectly explains the fundamental mission of all art in general and of music in particular. Here is Master Wen speaking to his teacher Master Xiang:

> What I have in mind is not to strum the strings well, or to get beautiful sounds. What I'm looking for is something I've yet to find in my heart. How can the instrument resonate inside me from the outside? But after several years, one spring day, he was playing the second of the five notes corresponding to autumn in the Chang style. Suddenly a cool breeze sprung up. The plants and the fruits on the tree ripened fully: it was fall. Then he played his guitar in the Kiao style. A warm wind blew and everything was in bloom; it was summer. He plucked the Yu string, and snow and ice appeared, the waterways froze, so it was winter. He then plucked the Che string: the sun came out and the ice melted.

*Lie Tseu is a transliteration of the name Lie Yukou, who is considered the author of the Daoist book Liezi (The True Classic of Perfect Emptiness), which bears his honorific name, Liezi.

This is how music perfectly illustrates art as magic; it inspires no less than the impossible: white magic versus black magic. Nevertheless, music never seems to recall any moments of everyday life, which doesn't prevent its active presence from making our hearts sensitive to certain truths and helping us to experience them most deeply. They are our suddenly opened being, which doesn't prevent the truths that are brought to our hearts by its active presence from helping us to live more intimately. They are our suddenly opened being, from within our actions; they help to transfigure our most mundane knowledge into grace, dream and revolt. They open our consciousness to the time they command.

For a long time I wondered what the reason for this was, without being too sure of my answers, until one day I realized that the question was the only one that mattered: To make music, what would it really be, if not to take the risk of remembering nothing of the present, so that the present would emerge precisely in a rapture that reveals eternity? When I play a piece of music—a piece by Brahms for example—I try to make myself his contemporary, and him my contemporary of, so that the nature of his notes, far from preceding me, is ahead of me. They lead me to an elsewhere that denotes the sojourn of the Absolute, an elsewhere that has no place, that is as much there as it is here; an elsewhere that makes the world present to me in its solar being and its dazzling becoming. To perform Schubert in this precise sense, I dare say is to remember as much as it is to anticipate—a way to remember the future, to make it so that time, in the advent of its full presence, suddenly restores life to all lost paradises and all paradises yet to come. As I reflect on the nature of the links uniting the present, memory, and future, I must keep in mind the imperious nature of the oblivion that discreetly governs this trinity.

Are you prone to nostalgia?

Not in my personal life. I live in the moment. It's a gift from childhood that I keep and nurture. I am never surprised by ruminating on what has happened or become sad about what no longer exists. I try to persevere in what gives me joy, in the path that gives concrete form to the project that I am leaning on and that I am trying to live with intensity. As an epigraph in one of my notebooks I wrote down the reply that the pianist Magda von Hattingberg made to Rilke after she had read his *Letters to a Pianist:*

> People claim something instead of being there, like the sun or a flowering tree, like a landscape that lets people grow without asking "What will you give me in return?" Perhaps you have never known anyone who has become rich in the "blessedness" of just being, who has found in it what he needed for fulfillment, because he himself was the promise and fulfillment of his own existence.

This attitude requires an attention span that music and its study increase tenfold, and it changes the way life is perceived. I have embraced this phrase: "Paradise is wherever I am." I work to make it truly so. I don't project myself into a distant future that is not yet real. I prefer to devote my thoughts to the present, to the here and now, so that I don't lose anything, not even a crumb, even when the sentimental or geographical landscape that I'm traveling through is less enjoyable and less conducive to pleasure.

At the very beginning of my career, I was asked: Where do you want to be in ten years? Are you interested in working with conductors? In fact, all I could think about was digging deeper into myself, as a person and as an artist. And the way that I got there didn't matter. I told myself: God knows where I will be in ten years. Trust your intuition and desires. Respond to your calling. Let music set the rhythm of your life and inspire its tempo. And yet, how can we not love nostalgia in the fruits it produces? In literature, and certainly in music. The Portuguese have a word to translate this feeling, *saudade*, and a music for to express it, *fado*. Cesária Évora sings this subtle blend of nostalgia, melancholy, and hope with great aptitude, and the essence of this music brings me back to that of Brahms, to his *lieder* of incomparable evocative power and sadness, since *fado* has its roots in the same compost. Etymologically, nostalgia comes from the words *nostos,* return, and *algie*, which means sorrow. It means homesickness. For the Greeks, nostalgia was the illness of return. The Romantics expanded its meaning to include regret. Regret for past happiness, lost love, and moments of happiness. Nostalgia no longer encompasses the strict desire to return to the homeland, to the mother landscape, but the passionate desire to see again, to relive, and sometimes to see at last—it's the nostalgia for paradise lost that we all carry inside. It's both a return in time and a return in space.

Romantic music gave extra emphasis to this extremely sensitive string, and there are countless adagios that plunge us into that sad and delicious saudade, that feeling of irrevocable loss but that writes, composes, admits, and recreates what has vanished. Obviously, because it crystallizes the widest possible range of feelings and sensations, which it endlessly juxtaposes, contrasts, harmonizes, or makes discordant because it is the preeminent source of the deepest tenderness and the most heart-breaking regret, nostalgia constitutes the bass line, a continuous bass of musical creation. It has the power that has inspired most composers of all kinds of music to act as a catalyst for our emotions. I would even say that music is the language of nostalgia. It stirs in us the fiber of desire in its most hidden facets, at the deepest level of our psyche. It reveals the imprint of the hours we have lived—the trace of our time on this earth. Nothing better than music expresses its poisonous charm, the immense octave of emanations it encompasses. Nothing better than nostalgia illustrates this truth spoken by Lévi-Strauss: "Only music can unite the senses with intelligence. Musical joy is the joy of the soul, invited for once to recognize itself in the body."

How would you define the intimate way you experience music? I know you've given a lot of thought to Armel Guerne's book, *The Insurgent Soul,* the complete writings of this member of the Resistance on German Romanticism. Wasn't it Armel Guerne who wrote that so-called classical music today is aimed at those who see life as a struggle for fulfillment against this demoralizing emptiness that leaves everyone like a piece of meat endowed with reflexes, once they have forgotten their soul, once they have abandoned their dreams—a risk and a journey, in the sense that Schubert experienced it, but a journey full of uncertainties.

Yes, it's an inner journey, a journey to recapture time, accompanied by the sensual experience of love for life. It is the experience of happiness if not joy. The poet and musician Orpheus sought to recapture Eurydice and the golden times he spent with her. Proust, in search of lost time, suggested music as the source of his richest memories, even more than the olfactory memory, the famous little madeleine.* Do you remember "Vinteuil's sonata" that Proust mentions in *Swann's Way*? It's a fictional work of course—and how clever to thereby allow everyone to find its correspondence with their own favorite pieces of music! But this work, with its famous "little musical phrase," its profound resonance, compels each of its listeners to listen to his own emotions, to be aware of the intimacy of his soul. This is exactly what I experience with music. As Proust said when he experimented with it on Swann, music "opens the soul wider," allowing access to the invisible reality of the world, to its vibration—the vibration of feelings.

Music for me is the experience that I live, that I make, of the reality of the unseen world. It is its tone. It opens its door for me, to which it is the key. Ever since I was a child, I've been delighted that the graphic sign indicating the pitch of the notes at the beginning of the staff is called a clef. The key of G, the key of F . . . Each soul has its own sound envelope that corresponds to a particular music and the unique sound of an instrument that reveals it. I was moved to tears the first time my mother read Baudelaire's poem to me for the first time. I was twelve or thirteen. I was working on a piece by Rachmaninoff. I was overwhelmed by a storm of emotions—as I often was—that I couldn't contain. In this feeling of helplessness, I bit my lip. She didn't say a word but opened *Flowers of Evil* and she read me these verses of Baudelaire's poem "Music:"

---

*Small spongy cakes, known for their seashell-like shape and iconic "hump." In France, a "madeleine de Proust" is a common expression referring to a smell, taste, or sound that dredges up a long-lost memory. In his book, Marcel Proust uses the madeleine as the trigger for nostalgia.

I feel vibrating within all the passions
Of a ship in distress;
The fair winds or the storm and its convulsions
Over the deepest gulf
Cradle me. Other times the flat calm, is the large mirror
Of my despair.

Finally, whatever anger, suffering, or revolt it suggests, music soothes these paradoxical emotions because it acts as a catharsis, a liberation of affects. What I like about music is that it keeps me on the side of life. In the eternal moment of a vital impulse—even when it speaks of death. I'll end with a quote from Vladimir Jankélévitch, because there isn't a word in there that I wouldn't make my own:

> Music transports and holds the musician in a kind of eternal present in which death no longer matters; better, it is a way to live through the unbearable part of eternity. My music, even when it seems funereal, like Chopin's, doesn't really speak to me of death, music speaks only of music.

Finally, music chooses all feelings and doesn't favor any one of them. It leaves me with a delicious, fruitful ambivalence, the ambivalence that is in my nature.

Are you trying to find a golden age again through music, if it is that key you describe so well?

I read a study about the relationship between the mother and the newborn, which has been confirmed by recent advances in neuroscience. It was about the child's earliest relations with the world from the mother's womb. The study emphasized the importance and primordial effect of the mother's voice during the prenatal period. It would be the first music heard by the child, its first relationship with the outside world, a relationship of tenderness and trust, and total surrender. The mother's voice is engraved in the child's memory long before her face. It is said that at birth, the baby can recognize its mother's voice among all others. Studies have also been done on the effect of a change of vocal tone on the child. A mother was asked to speak to her child by changing her usual way of speaking and addressing the baby in a monotone. The child then turned away from the mother. They realized that what the child liked, and what he was looking for in the mother's voice, was its singular, unique music, which consisted of musical modulations and intonations. I was very moved by this discovery. I loved and still love my mother's voice and listening to her speak. That lilting, modulated, soft voice. So to answer your question, it's not impossible that I found it in music, the one whose key I was looking for. Perhaps music is the transposition of that feeling of ideal fusion, that time of innocence and wonder of childhood. I recall being greatly moved by Proust's very apt words, when he mentioned the voice of his mother to whom he was so attached and sensitive: "I wondered whether music might not be the unique example of what might have been—if the invention of language, the formation of words, the analysis of ideas had not intervened—the means of communication between souls."

Music is mysterious, both light and deep, attuned to tears and joy—a reflection of life and mirror of the Absolute. Contrary to

Tolstoy's assertion, Jankélévitch claimed that music isn't so much inexpressible as it is ineffable. Is music for you an action in which intelligence has to prevail?

Music, as I've said, has nothing intellectual about it, and I often rebel against its classification in the context of activities reserved for the elite. There is nothing intellectual about it because it speaks primarily to the soul and the body and, thus, it eludes concepts that are too poor or too narrow to define it. Do you remember what Nietzsche wrote to his colleague, Franz Overbeck—Nietzsche who had dreamed of becoming a musician and for whom music was the pinnacle of language, "The animals with whom he was speaking, seeing his frustration, invited Zarathustra to abandon speech. He must learn to sing, as Socrates did at the time of his death. Ideally, the thinker must dance what he wants to say." When someone "makes" music as a profession, when it's more than that, a vocation, when you have a score in your hands whose essence you have to reveal to your audience, whose presence in the world is at that moment, you can't just study musical technique—music theory and practice. One must try to listen to everything that makes up the composer's universe, to learn about it, to establish the relationships between the society in which he grew up, the musical forms that were fashionable at the time, and his own perception as expressed in his works, but also to understand what his music contains that is absolutely unique, that transcends us, that overwhelms us. A serious study of the work is essential. Read the books that have been written about him whether their authors are musicologists, poets, philosophers, artists, painters—all those who tried to penetrate his mystery in the same way the alchemist sought the Philosopher's Stone. For the performer, it's a matter of transforming these strange signs written in black on staves into a narrative, of giving it voice, but also of making its author present during the performance of the work. As you read through these commentaries one by one, they offer some keys. All these spirits, most of them the artists themselves, heard and understood secrets while studying the work, and they had the grace to reveal them to us. You'd have to be terribly pretentious not to listen to them. If not all, at least some. A great musicologist is like a great musician. He can only strengthen a vocation, especially for a young performer. He doesn't close any door to the future: he opens them all. What I mean by this is that he never imposes any rule, because he takes care not to destroy what is the source of music: creative freedom. His example is not an end but a threshold where the adventure can resume. Everything that is said is only an observation—the observation of what is, never of what should be. That's the job of the interpreter, who is the only one capable of making others experience the living act of creation. That's why, once we've covered the widest possible circle of commentary and exegesis, it's necessary to detach ourselves from it, leaving both our own intuition and the listener's imagination free. I've always thought that a work carried its own keys within it. This brings us back to what we discussed earlier: music is a language that is far richer than any other language. We can read and study, but there will always be that dimension that eludes verbal description. As Frank Zappa said, "Writing about music is like dancing about architecture."*

*This quote (and variations on it) has been attributed to many different people; there is no general consensus of the origin.

The performer is there to reveal that dimension, to create a time outside of time—the time of inner life and pure feeling.

An example of a text that would have allowed you to overcome obstacles to your musical understanding?

There are a hundred! But I have one specific example. Thanks to Søren Kierkegaard I refined my technical ability and playing technique! Rehearsals are boring, difficult hours. You're confronted not only by the score and its difficulties, but also with yourself, with the tics you may have picked up in your attempt to overcome an obstacle more easily, and which need to be corrected with precision. One day I learned that the term "rehearsal" was one of the key words in Kierkegaard's philosophy. He focused on the etymology, which is the same for both Danish and German words. *Wierderholung** is perfectly clear. It is constructed with the verb *holen*, which means to look for again. What's implied here is that what needs to be repeated is not part of those things that a *person* can acquire once and for all. Repeating (rehearsing) doesn't mean trying to learn by heart. Repeating in this sense has an extraordinarily suggestive orientation. It is not a question of repeating something from the past but, on the contrary, anticipating something to come, and of always being in quest of it. This may appear anecdotal, perhaps even a little abstruse, but once I grasped Kierkegaard's idea, I was confronted by a completely new perspective, not only on the meaning of my rehearsals, but on the nature of interpretation—a permanent tension for the embodiment of

*Repetition.

music. That is why I never tire of playing the same concerto fifteen or twenty times during my tours. The work has no meaning unless the performer is able to give the impression that it was just created in that very moment. Sticking to a routine kills that freshness, and that's the worst thing that can happen to a performer on stage: a loss of sensory acuity. You have to stay alert, ready to walk on the edge of the precipice, even if it means cutting some technical corners. But a concert—that's life! And on stage as in life you have to know how far to go, and not too far. You have to leave room for the unpredictable. I took another big step in my musical education when I read this phrase by Heidegger in his book *On the Way to Language:* "Rhythm, in Greek, doesn't mean flux and flowing, but rather form. Rhythm is that which is at rest, that which forms the movement of dance and song, and thus lets it rest within itself. Rhythm bestows rest." This phrase can be compared to what Mallarmé wrote here: "I make music, and what I call music is not that which can be drawn from the euphonious juxtaposition of words, but from the beyond magically produced by certain arrangements of speech. Using music, in the Greek sense, basically meaning rhythm between relations." I then took a few hours to reflect in front of my keyboard and my scores, which I studied with each element of Heidegger's sentence. It was illuminating.

Let's get back to Schubert about whom we thought so much on the day we drove from Hanover to Bremen on a deserted, snow-covered highway, when it was impossible to tell the sky from the road, as if we had ourselves been trapped in the vertigo of *Winter Journey* . . .

I got to know him thanks to my teacher Pierre Barbizet, who taught me and prepared me for the entrance exam at the Paris Conservatory. He also made one of the finest recordings of some of his works. I was eleven when I met Pierre Barbizet. My teacher, Jacqueline Courtine, who had raised me from the status of little girl to that wondrous one of musician, had contacted this pianist whose name inspired the greatest respect and admiration among the students and teachers at the conservatory in Aix-en-Provence, where I was enrolled. There was a wonderful empathy between him and the music. Later, although I liked listening to Schubert's music—performed by Barbizet or in an equally marvelous organic way, Horowitz—I didn't yet foresee myself tackling his repertoire. There is an age for every musician, an age when one's curiosity about a composer grows sharper, when one begin to understand better what he is saying, to find personal resonances in his work, and echoes that one would like to translate in turn.

Schubert interested me, from an interpretative point of view, in the way he introduced the entirely metaphysical notion of time into his music and thus the theme of memory. We talked about this a while ago. I started thinking about it in 2003, when I was working on the concept for my record *Credo,* in which I wanted to create a resonance between a piece by Arvo Pärt, based on Bach, and the first Prelude from *The Well-Tempered Clavier.* I wanted to compose a set with this record that would abolish distances with notions of past, present, and future. No matter which piece you listen to, you find yourself in the same moment, in a play of mirrors, inside time itself, in its continuous, reversible flow. It's also a labyrinthine journey, the solution to which only the listener has through the themes of humanity: pain and suffering, but also joy and redemptions. All so many Schubertian themes.

Lastly, Schubert's works beautifully illustrate the essence of music, as described by Jankélévitch: "In music and in poetry what is said remains to be said, to speak and tirelessly and inexhaustibly to say it again." It seems to me that this creation that feeds on itself while constantly transforming itself, and which is also the principle of memory and recollection, defines that of Schubert. Schubert composed and, in the performance of his own compositions, he reinvented the music at each stage of his creative development—this is a lesson for the performer and interpreter that I am. Another point, among many others, that attracts me in his music: he wrote for the piano as much as he wrote for the voice. He considered the piano to be the alter ego of the voice, and it's an incredibly inspiring point to have to make the piano sing. To give to sound a human vocal range. Finally he has a duality that moves me. I've always been fascinated by the theme of the double that Schubert developed in his work, a theme he took from the work of Heinrich Heine. I so often feel like a double myself! I felt this way so strongly in my childhood! We can hear this duality in his music—a continuous overlapping of light and shadow, of happiness and melancholy, of bucolic and fantastic, of nostalgia and foreboding. All the variations of the soul in one way or another. We also see in it the full duality of time—memory and forgetting, and life and death, that death which had set the date of its rendezvous with him very early on, something Schubert knew. He evokes it in his letters in a very touching way. We hear both the pain and the consolation of pain. And then there's his acute sense of friendship, which extends to his love of nature, landscapes, and the elements that make them up. This affection and boundless tenderness can be heard in his works, especially in his *lieder.* He has a cheerfulness that results in the rarest of combinations, a music that is both extremely learned and "popular." Finally, Schubert is—historically speaking—a prelude to Brahms.

7

APPROACHES TO ROMANTICISM

Let's talk about Brahms, who has been and still is, I believe, one of your favorite composers, if not your favorite. Why are you so drawn to him, to the point of making him a character in your last book, *Return to Salem*? You wrote that you were struck by the fact that:

> *Brahms is most often treated not only in terms of clichés, the very nature of which is to reassure those who cannot undertake the journey with their heart as their compass, but also in terms of the worst prejudices, spread by his many enemies, who often secretly admired but spoke enviously of the resources of a breath that was openly denied to them. Thus, nothing has ever seemed to me more out of place than to repeat, as if the effort of repetition were to create a truth, that Brahms was the first of the second class of geniuses; nor have I ever accepted that people persist in portraying him as the epitome of the unaccomplished or academic man: a sentimental, cynical German, sexually impotent—worse, musically impotent.*

> *In short, a cyclone frozen in formulas. If Brahms continues to be played every night, if the most inspired performers of every kind, from soloists to conductors, from orchestral musicians to those who practice the very difficult art of chamber music, feel that they have grown by his approach, it's primarily because he is a double for music lovers, whose voices he was able to make sing, whose silences he was able to collect. For my part, what I admire about him, is this intense inner life, this continuous outpouring of emotion, carried by a science that doesn't stop at itself, nor at the desire to test its limits; this way of grasping the mystery of time, of unwinding it in reverse, according to the point of listening where one is situated—as if, in the end, one remained on the threshold; and as if, from the beginning, one had overcome almost all obstacles.*

I am glad that after Schubert, and only after Schubert, you are asking me about Brahms, because it is true that this composer has become a friend, a fellow traveler, a master of musical thought. After Schubert, Brahms. But before Brahms, Schumann, who was his teacher. And with him again, we find the principle of the double and otherness that would eventually draw me to Schubert. Sometimes Florestan, sometimes Eusebius.* Schumann was the musical symbol of this division, if not of this divergence like no other. Both model father and suicidal victim of rage, he tore things apart with the piano and the orchestra, shattering harmony with uncertainty. In his own way, Brahms was also a man with a "double" his entire life. Perhaps it was this characteristic, apart from their shared genius

*These are the names Schumann gave for the two extremes he identified in his personality. Florestan was outgoing and vigorous, Eusebius represented his introspective and morose side.

and common vibration of music that made them recognize and love each other.

Brahms, a dual being?

Sure. Who was more classical by being more romantic? Who was more collected by being more lyrical? Who was fresher and more naive by being the most erudite of all? These contradictions are revealed in his life, in which he was alternately almost completely withdrawn from the world and deeply involved with others, on the edge of love itself and yet always in love, nostalgic and conquering—the embodiment of Hoffmann's reveries in *Princess Brambilla*, where a young German artist, sitting at the Caffè Greco next to the charlatan Celionati, transposes one by one all the glitter of the Roman carnival into the inner sky of feeling. We find this duality again in his lieder. Inside each lied I can hear different voices: a mother speaks to her daughter, a lover confides her heart's desires, a lover expresses his anguish in a style that is sometimes elegant and sometimes farcical—think of *Vergebliches Ständchen*, a song that is as funny as it is popular. This feature allows each lied to be the scene of a pocket opera. The singer plays all the roles, but the contrasts between her characters are reflected in the interplay between voice and piano. The main theme of these lieder is love. But love with a wider scope than just young people.

In your opinion, how does Brahms define love?

In a way that certainly brought him very close to me and gave me the feeling of having a Siamese twin soul. For Brahms, love is "the" supreme emotion, the universal emotion. All human effort should be directed at dissolving into it at every opportunity. For him, love, like music, is above all a life's work. Far from icy bourgeois conventions and commercial interests, love appears in all its luminous evidence, in all its urgency, and the soul suddenly shines through; it gives beauty all its meaning, and the soul then throws itself naked into dizzying ecstasy. From there its unique risk carries it away. What's left? Hardly anything, in the scorched notes, a few flashes, a few obscure traces like those mysterious traces of lightning that leave nothing of the storm; a few signs whose meaning we don't understand, but which we nevertheless feel charged with a heavier, more pressing significance.

This was Brahms's experience for we know that he never married or had children, though he had the passion for it. Famously, he left a circle of his admirers to play merry-go-round with wide-eyed kids gaping at wooden horses or to go be with his good students whom he wanted to reward. Knowing this, it should no longer come as a surprise that the most recurring story told in the lieder—"Liebestrau," "Sommerabend," and "Der Kranz"—is that of a mother advising her daughter to leave the man she loves because he has betrayed her, to which the young woman replies that her love is intangible, and that she preferred him in his unhappiness to living without him and forging false joys. And then we'll say that Brahms was impotent, depressed, and gloomy! That's the spirit! He gives us two voices; he holds the contradiction. In the end, it becomes one song, with its nuances shimmering in the background. A great art that has the merit of knowing how to make us forget, as in "Wiegenlied," a lullaby that is both a declaration of love to the mother and to the baby, and which Brahms gave as a gift to the singer Bertha Porubsky, a woman he had courted and who had just given birth to her second child. Similarly, how can we fail to appreciate "Meine Liebe ist grün," which Brahms composed using the light verse of his godson, Felix Schumann, who was suffering from tuberculosis, and was the son of his mentor Robert and his love Clara. "Von ewiger Liebe" recounts the nocturnal ballad of two lovers in a desperate love affair. The man doesn't believe it. The woman replies that yes, love is stronger; a dialogue suffused in chiaroscuro that states, in the middle of the night, that the night is also a place of terrors to be tamed. This is answered by "Alte Liebe," or the evocation of a love that has fled and is all the sharper because of it.

To you, is Brahms still revolutionary in the sense of how the individual was perceived in his time? We know to what extent the French revolutions of 1830 and 1848 left their mark on all Europe, combining political action with poetic intent. We also know that Gambetta's* motto was: "Hope is forbidden to anyone."

Yes, Brahms is the preeminent revolutionary. His challenge is a challenge to death. It's proof that the present can be experienced with an intensity that equates man with creation, through the participation of all the senses. For those who know how to listen, a Brahms concerto can lead to a trance much more effectively than techno can. Joy, too. This is a false problem. Brahms,

*Léon Gambetta, French republican statesman who organized the resistance during the Franco-Prussian war.

like all artists, combines revolution and reconciliation in the same movement. He does not fight against this world, he carries and completes it. He saves it.

You are an interpretive performer of romantic composers. Historically we know that Romanticism can be summarized along three axes: the rights of the self (or the emancipation of the sociable, reasoning, and reasonable ego), the return to nature (with nostalgia for a lost sense of oneness and the cult of ecstasy that would restore innocence), and finally, the cult of passions and feelings, with a taste for dreams, for elsewhere, and no less for the Absolute. Would you define yourself as a Romantic?

It all depends on what you mean by the word when you ascribe it to someone, artist or no. If it's a vaguely idealistic person, no. If Romanticism is a way of life, a struggle for fulfillment, going for what's essential, and going with naked heart and open hands, no matter what, but going for it, then yes! It's certainly a constant risk to yourself and those around you. Without that, what's the point of living? My definition of happiness? To surrender all fear. The first Romantics—Kleist, Novalis, Hölderlin—spoke vehemently like rebels. They fought for what makes us live in truth. They warned their contemporaries who were busy building the society that we live in today, a society in which it is impossible to breathe. Each in his own way wanted his heart to be a faithful and exact image of his soul, which has nothing to do with anything but love. I understand love as the desire that changes the world.

Life draws its energy from feeling in love. For my part, I am in a constant state of passion. In any case, no passion, no music. Music is a passion that has found its rhythm. But be careful, the love I'm talking about is not necessarily love for an individual. It's rather love for life itself, in its most mundane and wondrous reality, which gives a sense of wholeness, an echo of the love we experience with a kindred spirit. I fall in love when I see animals frolicking in nature—the beauty of their bodies, their suppleness, their zest for life—or when I look at a mountainous or snowy landscape. Then I feel fulfilled beyond words.

Instead of seeing classical music as a remnant of the cultural world designed to flatter the listener, you believe that this can be a vehement demand to testify to our presence, our humanity. Not only as if we were dealing with a fleeting harmony, but also with the tearing at its heart. Is there a way to be a Romantic in the twenty-first century that is extremely modern?

Perhaps. Or at least, there is a common atmosphere, a look, an attitude. Again there is no recipe. Romanticism is a way of being, not a method. That would be terrible by the way; it would be the negation of everything this movement produced. To be a romantic, perhaps, is to keep one's eyes wide open, aware that if those who claimed to be such felt on the threshold of catastrophe, we have crossed it. What generations of people have feared, we are about to to experience by accelerating it. It is a matter of pride. To be a romantic is to refuse to indulge in thoughts of doom, whatever they may be. They flatter our cowardice, and that's intolerable. I've gradually learned to say yes to life. An unreserved but clear yes. Loving life is much more demanding than complaining about the slightest scratch. If I should live much longer, I'll tell you what it means to be a romantic: to wish that "the child's voice in him never be silenced, may it fall like a gift from the sky offering to dried-out words the brilliance of his laughter, the salt of his tears, his all-powerful savagery."

Aren't these last words, written some time ago by the novelist Louis-René des Forêts, a bit exaggerated?

No. They are simply in proportion to the danger, to its magnitude. We can't face the storms of the future by retreating into nooks and crannies, content to praise the small, the trivial, the silly, and I say that without disdain for the small. The fate that our pride has forged is far more tragic, and the answers to it much more demanding. You asked me if I was a Romantic? Let me be more precise. If I am, I would like it to be in the sense of Beethoven, perhaps the most romantic of musicians. To express, as he did, a desperate hope, driven by an anguish that demands it. Like him, I want to rethink the world with the magical will of its salvation; to restart the conquest of one's "cosmic" self for everyone. This is what Beethoven's music achieves: It opens up to us the possibilities of a limitless being, instead of reducing us to the dimensions of the cramped reality we create. "I have never made my peace with the *Pastoral Symphony* into which I have the impression Beethoven poured everything that was vulgar, facile, and childish in him (and that was a great deal), so as to have done with it once and for all," Samuel Beckett wrote. Then, in another letter he enthusiastically spoke of the Symphony No. 7 whose sound surface is "devoured by huge black pauses." Beethoven's romanticism? It is on the one hand to say "No"; on the other to say "Everything is possible." Here and now. And now or never.

What answers does Romanticism promise?

To each his own, according to his own talent. Poetry for some. Charity for others. For me it's music. It forbids me from playing so I can watch myself narcissistically in the mirror or perform a few tours de force, to try to dazzle the public with demonstrations of virtuosity—what Flaubert imagined that Emma Bovary dreamed of. I detest tours de force. I play for each and every listener. I say everyone, truly, and not all, because everyone has his or her own life. So I try to offer each one the means of rediscovering themselves by establishing a dialogue between the two of us. I don't cheat. The moment I step on stage, nothing exists anymore. It's an unprecedented face-to-face encounter, for which I feel I have only one option: to risk everything for everyone. You have to play as if the future of the world depended on it. And after all, why not? Who knows? It's one of those mysteries that eludes us but we have to make it happen. We have to make the impossible happen with all its risks and perils. I guess that's what "being a romantic" is all about. And so-called Romantic music is my preferred medium for achieving this, but there's nothing exclusive about this choice. Every piece has its own character. All great works, with their own nuances, force us to go beyond, to transcend our limits.

We'll never be finished, and at the end of our lives, we'll probably be sad that we didn't have enough time to devote to this and that, and already . . . to Bach, and to what he reveals: "the architecture of our fragilities" (Emil Cioran), as well as "the rainbow of the voices of souls and angels" (Jean-Paul de Dadelsen).

Are there halls or auditoriums that are more conducive than others to this exchange that you seek between each of your listeners and yourself? Do you have a favorite hall?

There are halls whose acoustics are better than others. Technical mastery has perfected this aspect of concert halls, but the ideal auditorium will never exist, because it's nothing without an audience. It is the audience that gives meaning to what you play. Consider, for example, the enthusiasm of the audience at La Roque d'Anthéron, whose auditorium is nothing more than nature. This open-air setting was the scene of memorable concerts, out-of-this-world moments, and rare happiness. The auditorium and the piano are only means: what they produce is beyond. It's in the rapport between an emotion that transcends the performer and the people who share it with her. German audiences are very receptive as are Italian audiences. And nothing is more amazing than the Japanese hall. The reactions there are so intense! Music is undoubtedly the most complete of the arts. At the height of emotion, the most contradictory emotions, there is no good or evil. There is music that is played with heart or music played without it. It's like making love to the moment. And this relationship allows a glimpse of eternity from time to time. Sometimes I tell myself that music has fairy powers; it's from a time that makes us forget. Intellectually, it only takes its power from sensibility; it appeals equally to body and mind, passion and contemplation. Without music, we would be deaf to silence. Without it, we would be like those inhuman beings described by Plato, when he speaks of the birth of the Muses. Before the Muses were born, nothing had any meaning; the moment they appeared, humanity was able to move forward. Where I'm concerned, I feel the music physically. It goes right through me. It doubles my body and gives me more than the spirit of things; thanks to it, I suddenly penetrate the invisible.

Now I understand better why you recorded Beethoven's *Tempest*.

I am convinced that the works of Beethoven—which, for my part, I always perform as if they had just been written because their youthful spirit is so far ahead of our thinking and insists on being more modern today than most fashionable music—speak louder than ever; his struggles and revolts have become our own. Our time has given them a vital urgency, perhaps even more urgent than his. In the name of the purity he placed at the heart of music. Beethoven rejected the compromises of his time, which he saw as a betrayal of the essential—what would he say two centuries later? If we listen deeply, his music continues to offer answers. It teaches us to choose love over hate, joy over distress, but also absolute freedom over voluntary servitude. It's beauty, all beauty and nothing but beauty. In general I don't think that the problem is to pit the old against the new. It's a debate that, under the pretext of excessive clarity, runs the risk of obscuring what is eternal in the past and what is perishable in the present—or, if you prefer, what is lasting, but in the making, in the everyday event that almost everyone invariably misses at the moment.

Did you feed your love of romanticism with anything other than music? You who write—we will revisit this—which authors have shaped your knowledge and appreciation of this artistic movement?

Of course there is Novalis. I would even say that Novalis came first. For him, only the poet can communicate with nature and become nature itself, without the risk of becoming a passive actor or totally dependent on it. But this union doesn't necessarily lead to a series of verses. The Poet thus has the chance to become a universal being. In the unfinished part of *Heinrchi von Ofterdingen*, the hero becomes a flower, an animal, a stone, a star. Novalis's sense of wonder was not an escape from life, but the conviction that life itself is a series of wonders. It's a completely contemporary mistake to assume that enchantment is a condemnation of reality. On the contrary, those who love life deeply can continue to do so provided that they see in it the expression of a thousand strange and contradictory impulses contributing to the creation of a unique beauty whose consciousness is as mysterious as the whims of elves and fairies. This is exactly why Novalis loved death, which he saw as just another transformation, the most extraordinary of all transformations. He would not have understood the label of morbidity that a certain critic scornfully applied to him. He felt that dreams, love, contemplation of nature, illness, and death all participated in the same union of self and nonself, which is the highest consciousness of poetry. In this world, where there is always an element of decay and destruction, the poet, by his secret action, appeared to him as the eternal spirit of resurrection, the true savior of matter. Thus this young man, who died at the age of twenty-nine on March 25, 1801, was one of the greatest prophets of the nineteenth century, the herald of a new era. I also see here correspondences with the shamanism I discovered among Native Americans, which I will soon discuss with you in greater detail.

Is Novalis the only romantic that has inspired you?

No, of course not. All the poets of romanticism have influenced me, each with their own unique note, because from Shelley to Leopardi, from Aloysius Bertrand to Gérard de Nerval, the whole of Romanticism has sought to reconcile the soul of the world and that of the poet who sings it, with the aim of becoming the world in turn, and if possible by new means: The prose poem, the use of drugs, the exaltation of dreams, and the search for a meeting point between here and elsewhere, between what belongs to this world and what belongs to it—night, love, and their revelations, whatever the price to be paid for them. Its time resembles our own. In a time that has seen the ruin of beliefs and the major disruption of ancestral ways of life and the rise of cities, the proletariat and scientific discoveries such as the explorations of the most remote lands, poetry and music, have for the first time in centuries, found their value as a counterworld, or a world in itself.

In France, if Victor Hugo's disciples made poetry a religion, Baudelaire made it a faith. Rimbaud read and admired him. When he spoke of him, he rightly called him "a true god!" Rimbaud took the poetic thought of his elder and pushed it to the limit, to the limits of what can be said. For Baudelaire, *Les Fleurs du mal* was a poetic volume of totality or, to put it another way, a treatise on thought, in versified and therefore musical form. At the end of his adventure, Rimbaud successfully created a poem that was no longer philosophical, but went beyond thought and its categories, by going straight to the motif and color, just as he invents music that harmonizes the cry and silence—which is why I never stop reading it and letting it penetrate me. Nevertheless, its stakes are not solely aesthetic; what's in play is not just the concern of a "poetic school." The great desire for conversion is at work in Western thought, where it's all about entering the new life that Dante, Baudelaire, and Rimbaud vowed: Baudelaire when he wrote that he hoped, thanks to God, that his mother might live to "enjoy [his] transformation," Rimbaud when he proudly chose his motto: "Change life." Their poetry goes far beyond aesthetics to call, by means of a superior verb, for the advent of a spiritual moment that no longer responds to a given religion, that no longer speculates on salvation, that relies on nothing but itself, at the risk of condemning these poets to wandering like cursed souls. This point is the guaranteed revenge of the critics.

With regard to Novalis, I would like to spell out how his romanticism, and after him that of Byron or Lamartine, this romanticism of the first days, was heroic. And I wholeheartedly embrace the idea expressed by Joseph Campbell when he said, "the artist is the best prototype of the modern hero." Wasn't the world to be reinvented, and happiness a new idea in Europe, as Saint-Just,* the archangel of the revolution, proclaimed?

*Louis Antoine de Saint-Just.

8

INTIMACIES

Does such a commitment, an artist's commitment to his art like you describe, leave much room for a personal life? Let's remember what the poet Henri Michaux said: "Music replaces individuals, mothers, wives, children, friends, in all their wonder, but from which we often unsuspectingly keep only that which expresses them by a marvelous subtraction of what is annoying because we wish to make it as harmless as those waves of joy that lift our hearts. Music, the deep, archaic axis that holds many axes together."

You could quote the end of the text: "An axis that precedes, we could say, ambivalence. Art that sings of the divine without having to believe in God, belong to a religion or adhere to a dogma." Now, if by "personal life" you mean "private life," there's little room, that's true. Nothing enriches my personal life more, my personal experience of this very moment among all moments, than my commitment to music. But my private life? What we prosaically call everyday life? So little space. Between rehearsals, concerts, world tours, the personal work of sight-reading and exercises, there is little time left in the day to devote to others, to the other. I am very grateful to my friends for their loyalty. They understand why I'm rarely available and how little time I can give them . . . "in person" as we say today. We talk on the phone, but we still have to calculate for time differences. Sometimes I forget to do this and I've called friends during the wee hours of the night, causing them to feel a vague sense of fear. What happened that I had to wake them up? With the person who decides to commit his or her life to you, with you, this lifestyle is actually a problem as soon as the artist's partner expects a "normal" couple's life with regular hours. Or when his love needs the carnal and constant presence of the other to express itself. I understand how a person can feel abandoned when they wake up alone every morning for weeks on end because the other person is running all over the world. I can understand how the despair of not being able to open your heart and share your day when you come home at night. And it can be frustrating, even hurtful, when you're on the phone and you don't feel that the other person is paying attention, fully receptive to your joys, sorrows, difficulties and hopes. This partner has to realize and accept that after a concert, that is the time when he or she can call because from the morning on, between meetings with the organizers, the conductor or the musicians, the rehearsals, then the performance itself, it is impossible to get a hold of us, and after the concert we are totally "empty." It's not an elegant way to put it, but it perfectly defines this feeling of hollowness, emptiness, and depression in terms of the loss of pressure that a concert performer feels. I've been on stage for two or three hours, I've given my all to the audience, and the music has exhausted me to the point where I experience that deep sorrow, sometimes accompanied by tears, that women feel after giving birth. A friend told me of her postpartum depression and while she was talking, I thought to myself, "But that's exactly how I feel after concerts." It's the feeling that a constitutive element of my personality has been taken away and nothing will replace it in the hours following this delivery to the world. There are also times when the current with the audience is so intense that it electrifies me for hours. Then I'm in a state of excitement and euphoria that puts me out of sync with the rest of the world—like that of students at the end of the final exam for their diploma. I'm gripped by an exhausting logorrhea for my listeners, be they parents, friends, or companions. A third person enters your life as a couple, invisible but tangible, like a lover, and who, like a lover, establishes the principle of a double life: the audience. It's the audience to whom we give ourselves on stage, it's with the audience that the music-listener couple, of which the performer is the link, is built. The audience is who you talk to in the evenings, who you share your life with when the tours and concerts begin. And sometimes we linger with the members of the audience after the show, at least with some of the most loyal ones, because they really feel what just happened, they prolong it, they tell you about it, and they've always been with you. Even if your connection with them is just about the music and your relationship with the stage and the piano, it's still intense. I have great friends among these devotees, even though I see them rarely and infrequently. During my concerts, I recognize faces, I see their smiles and little hand gestures, and to each of these strangers who have become so familiar and necessary to me over the years, I give everything the music allows me to give to them. I've said when everything in a concert is in tune with grace we are formidably, fiercely together. In those minutes when I face each of them, me on stage and they in the room, we are in communion—the same love flows through us. For a long time I thought that nothing in a love encounter outside of music could ever convey this truth. I was wrong, of course. What followed showed me how wrong I was. But what I was right about was that it's a mistake to believe that the emotion of the moment can be exported to other places, other times, other affects. Even when the temptation to violate this rule is strong, we must resist at the risk of falling into cruel disappointments.

And have you suffered?

I chose this life, or rather, it chose me. It has always been completely obvious and I never envisioned any other. Music is not a job for me, it's my life, my vocation, and I've always wanted to be faithful to the Romantic's method of embodying music in my life at every moment. This is another point that can create an imbalance in a couple, when one has a job and the other has a passion. For many, work is a constraint, or torture, as the etymology of the word suggests, and they find it hard to accept that it can be a source of infinite joy that we try to revitalize and renew infinitely. It's never a routine that you repeat at nine in the morning and put on hold at six or seven in the evening. It is a constant movement, a challenge, and a sometimes painful interrogation. Music inscribes me in a movement, a kind of fugue, from which I can't dissociate myself because, frozen, music dies, and I believe I will die with it, because it sets the tone for the rest of my life. I finally met the man who agreed to share my life with me, who understood that what I gave to music didn't take away from him, but on the contrary, it fulfilled me and allowed me to give more of myself to our relationship. He understands this all the more because he's an artist himself, has to move around and, as a photographer, has to practice his art in a *chambre noire** for his developments just as I need chamber music for my studies and rehearsals. Isolated from each other, we support each other's thoughts in this seclusion because we know the common meaning of our work. This creates a joyful phenomenon of spiritual transmission and the flow of thoughts, everything becomes light, and no part of this solitude is barren. There are no more of those painful complaints that I endured in love, and by that I mean all emotional relationships, relatives, friends, saying I was selfish or narcissistic, all confusing my person (from whom I also take everything) with the music to which I give my essential focus. In the end, my idea of love is such that for a long time I've preferred to live alone rather than having to be satisfied with half measures, if not permanent compromises—even if they're required in daily life when living as a couple. I agree. La Rochefoucauld said: "There is no such thing as a delightful marriage. But you will see that there are some good ones." Whether they are good, if not truly delightful, that depends on us. Like everyone, I know that love is not given and even though I have found it, it has to be earned every moment. As soon as you think you have love, you are on the verge of losing it, and if you don't take care of the other person's love, it's not

*Darkroom.

only his loss but also your loss. Love is not something you own like property, or something you can be sure will last, it's the most ephemeral part of our being; it needs to be strengthened every day. It's the work of a lifetime. A work that will not tolerate half measures.

What is your idea of love?

What I say about music I would also say about love. We cannot live on love alone. And we should not die for love either, and not a tragic death. We should only create to go beyond that death, and only stop creating through that death. To forge this ideal both in love and in music, I chose as my essential ally: Arthur Rimbaud. I still find it surprising that people still question his silence, without understanding that it is only the counterweight to his musical fairyland. For Rimbaud was first and foremost music, a "fabulous opera." Following his example, seduced by the magnetism that makes a few words the largest magnetic field available to us, if I want to find my way, like a compass dial, to the heart of what's essential, in love as in music, I read out loud again his ultimate promise, which answers to the name of genius. Everything is said in two sentences: "His day! the abolition of all sonorous and moving suffering in more intense music." And then: "His body! the dreamed-of release, the shattering of grace crossed by new violence!" Thus, a being will come along who will measure himself against the tragedy that is at the heart of our existence. He will cast off misery by the vision he gives himself of it in which he will see himself and humanity, but he won't stop there: Music will carry him along. Rimbaud describes this genius in advance: "He is love, perfect and reinvented measure."

Did you know that in 1875 after he stopped writing, Rimbaud took piano lessons from a teacher named . . . Louis Létrange? He played while his younger sister Vitalie sang. Vitalie wrote that he spent entire days working on it. After all, didn't he write: "For I is another. If brass wakes up a trumpet, it's not its fault. That's obvious to me: I witness the unfolding of my own thought, I watch it, I hear it, I make a stroke with the bow, the symphony begins stirring in the depths, or springs with one leap onto the stage."

Do you think it is possible to live up to such an ideal? And to live it for a lifetime?

Definitely, that is something that music teaches me every day. Music educated me as much as my mother did, because I left home quite young, as I said, to go to Paris and the conservatory. She educated me in a certain sense: She raised me. Bach, Mozart, Haydn, and more precisely and more specifically, Rachmaninoff, Brahms, and Chopin taught me life, and by working on their works, I constantly question them. They are the guardians and initiators who ceaselessly, inexhaustibly, remind me of the horizon and the source, of renewing and surpassing myself. Music proclaims, and will always proclaim the truth, because it proclaims the future. The work, humility, and listening that it requires to reach ecstasy should be applied in the same way to our loving relationships, whether as a couple or as friends. Like music—we must not imagine we can play a Chopin nocturne without having studied music theory and practiced our scales. And we can't lose sight of the fact that we are responsible for the love someone holds for us, once we have accepted it. This singular, unique love between two individuals, this miraculous love, is like the child brought into the world by a loving—and I stress this—an equally loving encounter. Would we even think of leaving this newborn child without care, affection, or food, and then blaming it for starving to death?

Yes, I've integrated love and music. In *Private Lessons,* where I talk about my romantic education, I mention the little film that I liked to project for myself at the conservatory before going to sleep. A seer was looking into a crystal ball; she rubbed it and suddenly the glass globe opened and poured out in the entire space, on every floor, floods of Bach for the desperate, Brahms for the lovers, Mozart for the spiritual, and Vivaldi for the joyful. I've always known that when I interpret a work on the piano, when I try to convey its mystery, when I finally succeed and unveil it in a kind of state of grace, it is love in whose eyes I look. That's what the works I perform most often teach me, and that's why I've chosen them. Finding the key to the works is also finding the key to love.

Nevertheless, I have to clarify a few things. In my opinion, love, in a general sense, doesn't exist. It's always a game between a "you" and a "me" that passion reveals in their uniqueness. To love, in this specific sense, is to be able to unfold according to the laws of life that best suit us. This is why love—not the cry of extreme suffering, nor the premonition of perfect joy, but a revelation that could be called feverish—is indeed the most powerful spiritual experience, the deepest form of knowledge, the release, in experience, of a transparency of being that must be held before us like the end of the road, however labyrinthine and shattered by storms it may be. What is love if not opening oneself to a fulfillment that desire contains and renews with the world; and, through this openness, to allow the dreamed-of infinite to embody itself in the finite person of the individual we choose? "I want you to be"—this is how love speaks, as Robert Schumann, Clara Schumann, and Johannes Brahms* spoke it in their works, each for the other.

Robert wanted his wife to be music herself, just as Clara wanted Johannes to be music, and for the latter to allow his two friends to be as they remain to us through their notes, in their intensity, proof of a love story that was unique, like all stories that seek to conquer and reach an absolute. In their own way, these musicians, whose inner space was a vertiginous risk, make us understand that love is an unfailing charity, the most intimate freedom of one toward the other.

Music has taught you about love and still does, certainly, but does it teach you about relationships?

Yes and no. Or rather no, and yes. Not because a person cannot live on music alone. I've been in that situation of emotional loneliness, which I've found to be a burden—a state that tells us something is missing. There's a sense of incompleteness. It's not the physical relationship that's missing; it's the heart-to-heart, soul-to-soul, trusting relationship. It's knowing that a being on this earth cares for you as much as you care for him and waited for you before he knew you, and waits for you to return when you are apart. It's knowing that you are . . . his favorite. But the desire to meet someone doesn't always bring about "the" meet-

*Brahms was in love with Clara, who was married to Robert.

ing, the one with your cosmic twin, your kindred spirit. So we can rush into a relationship on the wrong footing, thinking it's the right one, the only one, and, in short, find only desire, joy, pleasure, sex, and sometimes even self-esteem. This is not so bad, but it's not the essential for building that ideal love relationship called a couple.

Why do you mention self-esteem?

It's probably the most pernicious trap. It's love as bait. It's allowing someone to adore and admire you, and not responding to that with love but your self-esteem, which rejoices in a form of self-fascination or narcissism that can be self-destructive. That is why there are so many breakups, so much disillusionment, so much relationship-hopping. So much screaming and anguish, and so much loneliness. It's easy to understand Auden's wish: "*If* equal *affection* cannot be, Let the more *loving* one be me" (emphasis added).

And life as a couple?

I don't think there are any recipes for living together except the good old basic rules that are indispensable to any relationship: respect for the other person, respect for his or her freedom. On the other hand, there are a few things you can do to guarantee a disaster. For example, get involved with someone who doesn't listen to you or understand you. If you've made that mistake, it's because you didn't understand or listen to him either. If there were a recipe for the ideal life together, we'd know it by now, because people have been living, marrying, and having children for over three thousand years. And how could there be? Each of us is singular, unique, made up of thoughts, desires and impulses that we don't always know about ourselves. This mysterious compound meets another, equally complex, subtle and fragile. The combination of the two can be perfect or disastrous. Finally, there's the essential spark, Cupid's arrow, that first look when you know that everything is at stake, or has already been played out—the look that Vronsky and Anna Karenina exchange at the Moscow train station. As Anna walks away, she knows not to look back to see if Vronsky is following her with his eyes—something she is already sure of. She's aware of the consequences of moving her head in this way, their eyes meeting—the birth of an agreement and the sign of her consent to a forbidden love. If she does it, she will be lost and will have no power over her life or her feelings. And again I'm evoking a passion, a love frustrated by fate: Anna was married when she met Vronsky, at a time when divorce was unthinkable. But would they have loved each other so fiercely if it hadn't been forbidden, it hadn't been the pleasure if transgression? Then, as we've seen, there's the complexity of lives and professions, the imprint of a particular upbringing, the differences in each person. There may be resistance to the fusion of two souls. Finally, living as a couple means confronting the ideal with the rough edges of reality, the difficulties of daily life, the discrepancy that can arise between the moods of one and the other. We are not always in tune. Nevertheless, if there is no recipe, there are directions, and paths to follow. Music shows us them, as I said before—never take the result for granted, never neglect to strive to perfect your love. They are all revealed to us as well by poets, writers, and artists.

Who do you have in mind?

Nietzsche gave this splendid definition when asked what makes a successful couple. He replied, "A long conversation." That says it all. When I see those couples in a restaurant who are no longer speaking to each other, or those whose faces are buried in their cell phones, I repeat this philosopher's words to myself. Finally, I believe in an education for love. This education is given to us by example. I was fortunate to grow up in the shadow of loving parents. I had a mother and father who were a magnificent couple for a model. If we aren't nurtured by love from childhood—through example as I said, but also through literature, music, and poetry—if we don't forge an ideal for ourselves, then love will appear in our lives in its most frustrated form, the couple, which should be the most sublime form. Love with a capital L must exist before love. But how can it? We no longer love the world. We no longer love the future, we no longer love tomorrow. Can we love without this faith, without this trust? We no longer love others, we are afraid of them: Have you seen the people on the bus, on the train, in the subway? No one talks to anyone; everyone clutches their bags and collars. The other person is my fear.

You have no model, you say, but how do you know the truth of what you are describing?

Joy. Nothing is more terrible than to wallow in an unhappy passion, an unhealthy relationship that today's psychiatrists call "toxic." Joy, a joyful love, leads us to exchange and share. Here I am, obliged to give back to the one I love the freedom I have received from his love. I've been talking about the lessons of literature. It's time to render unto Caesar what is Caesar's. Time to repeat the words of Rilke, Samuel Beckett, and Henry Miller, that I've already quoted in my book *Private Lessons.* Rilke:

> *For this is the failing, if there is a failing in*
> *anything,*
> *Do not increase the freedom of the beloved*
> *With all the freedom you find in yourself.*
> *When we love we have to hold on this alone.*
> *To not let the one be the other.*

Samuel Beckett: "Her eyes opened and let me in." Henry Miller:

> I no longer look into the eyes of the woman I hold in my arms but I swim through, head and arms and legs, and I see that behind the sockets of the eyes there is a region unexplored, the world of futurity, and here there is no logic whatever . . . this selfless eye neither reveals nor illuminates. It travels along the line of the horizon, a ceaseless, uninformed voyager. . . . I have broken the wall created by birth, and the line of voyage is round and unbroken. . . . My whole body must become a constant beam of light, moving with an ever greater rapidity, never arrested, never looking back, never dwindling. . . . Therefore I close my ears, my eyes, my mouth. Before I shall have become quite a man again, I shall probably exist as a park . . .

Finally, to illustrate this quality of freedom that must be the very atmosphere of love, there is this passage by Stig Dagerman that I chose for the epigraph to my first book, *Variations Sauvages.*

> But from a direction still unknown to me, comes the miracle of liberation. It could occur on the beach, where the same eternity that so recently awoke my fear, now witnesses the birth of my freedom. What is the miracle made of? Simply: my realization that no power, and no person, has the right to make such demands on me that my desire for life disappears. For without it, what can exist?

9

MORE ON LOVE

You mentioned moments of loneliness. Are they frequent in the life of a concert pianist like yours? How do you get used to them?

Since I was twenty, I've been moving nonstop from one end of the planet to the other, always happy when I can set my bag down in my little farm in Salem between two tours. During these tours, you can feel alone psychologically, because you miss the people you love, but objectively, you are never really alone. Everything is in place from the moment you arrive until you get back on the plane, with people waiting for you, taking care of you, responding to your wishes. To tell the truth, I've only really experienced radical solitude in its essence, in two situations. Or rather three situations. In Tallahassee, when I was nineteen I tried my hand at the American adventure and found myself in this little city in Northern Florida. And I had no point of reference except music. I experienced many barren hours, saved only by the presence of Harvey, a husky German shepherd mix who was overjoyed to be able to roam the long, deserted streets of this suburb of an American city.

Harvey also connected me to my family through the memory of Rip, my grandfather's dog, whom I loved enormously, as I always did as a child whenever I came in contact with an animal. I traveled through this time as lonely sailors are forced to do. I armed myself against the attacks of doubt and emptiness, as they do against storms, by shutting down everything in my mind that could let them in. With Alawa, the she-wolf, I relived the evening when I met her and we became necessary, indispensable to each other.

The other moment of loneliness is on stage during concerts. I've already mentioned the tension, the energy, the strength it takes to play alone, to hold the whole hall and the quintessence of the music to which you give life—to make it say what you hear of the meaning it carries and which can still save us today, save us from sadness, vulgarity, and cynicism. Playing alone is an odyssey, a solitary climb up a mountain on a path that has never been opened. It's a harsh, almost religious experience. Every night, even if the program is the same, you have to reinvent yourself and strive to be what some performers have managed to embody: a saint, a saint in the order of spiritual voluptuousness. You must play with the fear—the terror—that the magic won't work or that you won't be able to stay in this movement rising to fulfillment—the fulfillment of the music and of yourself. There's no way around it, no mechanism to prevent failure. You can rehearse for days and hours on end, but if that little bit of inspiration is missing, that connection to the very mystery of music, the doors remain closed—you won't enter the infinitely suggestive world of music and you can't let anyone else in. You are alone, terribly alone during this exercise, and even more so when you fail.

And the third situation?

I was sick, so sick that I had to cancel a lot of concerts. I had to take a step back. The good thing was—you always have to find a good thing to stand firm in the face of adversity—I felt empathy for all those who had gone through this barren crossing and those who were still going through it. One day I stumbled across these words by Flannery O'Connor, which reminded me of this interlude of illness, which she considered as a kind of journey: "I have never been anywhere but sick. In a sense sickness is a place, more instructive than a long trip to Europe, and it's always a place where there's no company, where nobody can follow."

Did love inspire a particular record?

Absolutely. It's the record that I called *Reflections.* Why Reflection and not Love, since it's inspired by the love between Robert Schumann, Clara Schumann, and Johannes Brahms? I prefer the word *reflection* because it can be understood in several ways. There is the common meaning, thought—reflection as a result of the act of thinking—and for me, music is not separate from thought. It's a way to make the world *comprehensible,* to give it a *higher reason.* Music is certainly an art of sensitivity, but a sensitivity that ends in intelligence, as we say "to be of one mind with a person." Music is the expression of such a discreet understanding of life. The etymology of the word also indicates that it is a bending backwards (re-flexion), a bending that returns to its point of departure. All reflection draws the space of a circle, in which we travel a path, with a point of departure and a point of arrival.

But the love of the three musicians?

It is in this path and its completion: from Robert Schumann's love for Clara Schumann, through Clara Schumann's love for Robert Schumann, to Johannes Brahms's love for Clara Schumann. In other words, it's a record that begins with love and ends with love, through a relationship that may be complicated, but that also creates a coherent space. Despite the madness, despite the death, it's love that triumphs—the love that we hear in their music and that always tugs at our heartstrings. I wanted to show that while this love is not an easy path, it's not impossible either. Therefore we should not make a space for it in our lives but generously give it all space. In other words, the works that I play on this record are the height of sensitivity and thought. It forces us to ask questions about ourselves, the most important of which is what must love, what must fidelity, what must passion be, in order not to fall into their mutual destruction? Robert Schumann loved Clara Schumann, who loved Johannes Brahms, who adored both his friends. We could make this a story of a love triangle (the husband, the adulterous wife, the young lover), if not a sordid or farcical vaudeville show, whereas the music they composed shows that it was something quite different, that it was in fact the exact opposite: Their love bore fruit, it was creative, it expressed the hopes of love. Then there's reflection, in the technical sense of the play of light on mirrors: mirrors reflect. Jean Cocteau once quipped: "Mirrors would do well to reflect a little longer before reflecting my image back to me." Generously yield all space. For my part, what I wanted to capture were the reflections of Robert's, Clara's, and Johannes's music on each other. The interpreter is the mirror of the others, transmitting their brilliance. She lends them her life. More generally, I wanted to complete the trilogy initiated by *Credo*. *Credo* raised the question of faith in a world where no one believes in anything anymore, where chaos reigns—wars and catastrophes are everywhere—and the future seems uncertain, if only from an ecological point of view with—this should be repeated and repeated, nonstop—man's destruction of his own habitat and that of other species. A faith that doesn't test itself through doubt quickly threatens to become just another fanaticism, with all the known risks. This moment of doubt is what I wanted to point out in my recording that deals with death through the sonatas of Chopin and Rachmaninoff.

For what reasons?

I was sure that I had to do it in a kind of enlightened state. I was on tour in Japan, and I found out that my illustrious colleague, Maurizio Pollini, was dedicating an evening to playing Chopin. I went to hear him and during the concert, I don't know why, I was flooded by the presence of people I had loved and who had died. My great-grandfather and his slightly rough tenderness, who trustfully let me escape and entrusted me when I ran away to his dog, a dear friend, who took something of me with her when she left, something of my soul that I've never found again. I had this sudden epiphany, this sense of urgency: I had to play and record the *Funeral March,* and that, recorded with Rachmaninov's Second Sonata, would illuminate the dissonant chord of pain and life that death has laid down and that only death can resolve. The two sonatas of Chopin and Rachmaninoff would make this revelation tangible. The soul of true love would also be revealed there, as it is love that causes great pain as well. The heart knows nothing of the one who is no more, except that it repeats to itself: "He was," and: "He is no more." What, then, does music offer to our sorrow? Ineffable sadness: the beloved is a word inscribed by passion and erased by chance; fervent hope: those who die have not lived in vain, they fade into themselves only to live again in the body of the eternal spirit; a call, at last: Chopin and Rachmaninov, spanning the whole space of feeling, urge us to love life in others to excess; to seek salvation, if there is one; to make new beings of ourselves, to be perpetuated by a new love. Death, as we all know, is at the heart of life. Only love can enable our consciousness to grasp it and, after suffering it, to free itself from it.

Do you apply this "reflection" that you value so highly, this play of mirrors, to your life, to your various activities, which at first glance seem so paradoxical, so far apart?

I'm often asked why I founded a center for wolves, why I fight for ecological causes, why I wanted to do a concert on the theme of water and to include Mat Hennek's photographic work as if it were an installation, and why I write. It's as if they think that this overlap is absurd. Some people think that my foundation for wolves and my interest in mustangs has nothing to do with my work as an artist, or that my books have nothing to do with my musical research and I run the risk of being distracted by them. People also present me as an expert in animal behavior. But this title is a far cry from my activities at the Wolf Conservation Center, which began in 1999, first run with volunteers, then with professionals: There's a space between the specialist and the witness that only passion can fill.

I'm not a wolf specialist—is there such a thing as a human specialist?—except for the love I feel for them and the fact that I help to defend them. Specialists have the advantage in what they study; for my part, without ever sacrificing the rigor of a scientific approach, I have to admit that I am first and foremost haunted by the spirit of these animals, as magnificent as they are indispensable to the survival of the ecosystem. As a musician working to save wolves, mustangs and, through them, nature—especially for young people—I don't make a distinction between my various activities: They all originate in my feeling that life must be preserved and exalted, *despite any and all obstacles*. All these struggles, which I put on the same line, come from the same essence: that which makes me who I am. All my activities are unified—including writing. I make no distinction. It's always the possibility of saying the same thing with precise nuances. This thing, you could say, is the passion to exist, the urge to create an enchantment, to give oneself a universe more beautiful and more powerful than temporary misfortune. Or to inspire a desire, if not to make it more beautiful, at least to preserve it, to save it as it is. This was confirmed for me when I worked on Brahm's Second Concerto, a piece that is very difficult to perform and interpret requiring a high level of technique and an extremely delicate touch because in this concerto Brahms expresses his entire vision of the world.

This vision? An anxious fear for the future that is answered by a proposal for a return to beauty, love, and the love of beauty through the exaltation of nature. There is that idea of our intimate connection to the land where we were born and the sacred character of that land. Above all there is that idea that everything is connected, by invisible bonds, art, man, nature, and that it's in the harmony of the balance between the three that our happiness can be found.

Is there something specifically feminine about the way you play the piano?

When I think of pianists—a nonexhaustive list—I think, at random, of Alicia de Larrocha, Rosita Renard, Rosalyn Tureck, Yvonne Lefébure, Tatiana Nikolayeva, Brigitte Engerer, Elisabeth Leonskaja, Catherine Collard, Magda Tagliaferro or Marcelle Meyer, and of course Myra Hess or Wanda Landowska, are undoubtedly greater geniuses than a number of male pianists, perhaps because they also had to fight against prejudice! I won't forget that I was friends with Marie-Josèphe Jude at the conservatory.

And in your case?

In any case, there's something very personal about it. And since I'm a woman, that component certainly plays a role in my playing. One day, from a teenager who ran with horses, then with wolves, I transformed into a woman. And I began to realize the power my gender had given me to restore to music its power to heal bodies, souls, and the world. If I had to write my epitaph, I'd write: "Neither witch nor fairy, but both in their own right." A witch because of the deep intuition I have for the animal and plant world, something I learned to develop. It's a kind of instinct and innate complicity. As a child, I remember cutting into the trunk of an oak tree to mix the blood from my wrist with its sap. And sometimes when I'm walking in the forest with my dogs, it seems to me that the trees remember it, that they remember this fraternal pact. I often express my gratitude to them. I hug them and ask them to penetrate me with their strength. A fairy, too; through the power of music I experience these states of grace that sometimes occur on stage. I also have a tendency, and this might be a female trait, to play some works alone at home for a long time, before thinking of recording them—something in the nature of taming them, approaching them—stealthily like a wolf. As an example, the works of Johann Sebastian Bach. I wouldn't mind being told that I play Bach in a feminine way, if that view encompassed the nature of Bach's love, maternal in its preference for others over itself. Bach loved with all his being, in the most carnal, embodied way, so that, by erasing his name, he might forever give voice to something like the revelation of life, to us, like a woman to her child, which explains its universality; as if his music were the consciousness of music itself, its certainty and its promise. Perhaps no one, with the exception of Shakespeare, was able to transform every atom of the universe, all the brightness in the world, with such deep and intimate feeling. Bach is the composer who combines, in their truth, the plenary tenderness of prayer and the solitary echo of the divine like he did. In turn, he seizes space and turns it into an infinite curve; he takes time and turns it into future possibility; he grabs a dance and gives us an engagement to celebrate. He restores sight to us who see so poorly. We are given to believe that there are no limits with Bach, he urges us to find him on the same level, in that practice of love that holds the obligation for the living to expand their lives and bring them back to the hearth of the heart.

The urgency of the moment is no longer disputed today. It would be a mistake to see Bach only as a man of his time, a witness to his times—for Bach is yet *to come.* Even in his lifetime, he eluded his contemporaries, who saw him as a relic of the past, not a prophet for all time and all people. What would be more natural than to find him at the source of Liszt, Busoni, or Rachmaninoff? Bach was like an island in the middle of the stream; moored against the current, he felt nourished on the side of origin and carried along on the side of hope. Between these two boundaries is a symbolic path that is the signature of all existence. Bach was never torn apart. He knew how to build bridges. He shows us in a flash that has the clarity of transparency how to reconcile the sorrow of the days and the burst of light.

Now that I've finished this digression on Bach, and to return to your question, is there anything specifically feminine about the way I play? I would have to be able to say very precisely what in my life has shaped my nature. Was it my gender? My travels? My concerts? My encounters? My reading? What shaped me as a woman? I don't know. But I admit that I'm happy that I was born with this gender by chance. And I'm happy to talk about it, especially today, when the feminine is only allowed to express itself by airing demands, often violently. It is sometimes difficult to speak one's mind because artists are often ordered to take radical positions. But I refuse to be pigeonholed into the feminine category—or any other, for that matter. I am a woman, but also a musician, a writer, an ethologist, and an ecologist. In short a full-fledged person, not an organism from which this or that substance can be extracted. "Let's forget that I am a woman, and let's talk about music," retorted Nadia Boulanger, irritated that journalists always started their questions with this topic. What is important in the execution of a work is never the personality of the artist, except for his ability to open the soul of the listener—does he open his feminine side, his masculine side, his mystical side, his violence, or his tenderness? The possibilities are endless and the effect of listening is different for everyone, and who cares if the performer is male or female.

There's no denying that many works have been passed over in silence because they were composed by women. How do you get them out of the closet, where they've been carefully locked away, without dedicating a special section to them?

You can't fix one form of bigotry by perpetuating another! I am interested in these composers and their works. I hope they will be made known and studied in music conservatories around the world, and played by orchestras, especially if their works are noteworthy. The works of about seven hundred and seventy women composers have already been catalogued, from Hildegarde von Bingen, in the twelfth century, and Francesca Caccini, in the seventeenth, to Camille Pépin and the Finn Kaija Saariaho, our contemporaries, which amounts to some sixty individuals. Francesca Caccini was the first woman to have written an opera, and Barbara Strozzi was one of the first professional female composers. The Frenchwoman Élisabeth Jacquet de la Guerre, star of Versailles during the reign of Louis XIV, and the Marquise Hélène de Montgeroult, need no introduction. Legend has it that the latter saved herself from the scaffold by improvising on *La Marseillaise** before the revolutionary tribunal. As I studied this list I was quite struck by the number of English composers. I am very grateful to the harpsichordist Claire Bodin who invented a platform she called "Ask Clara," referring of course to Clara Schumann, on which this list can be found accompanied by the biography of each of the musicians. Claire also created a festival, "Présences féminines," to exhume their works from dusty library shelves. As we all know, music that isn't played doesn't exist.

Have you played one of them?

Absolutely. On my album *Reflection,* I chose three *lieder* by Clara Schumann sung by Anne Sofie von Otter, whose voice is admirably suited to the personality of Clara Schumann. Anne Sofie von Otter's phrasing is aristocratic without being haughty; it is set at a certain pitch from the start, in keeping with the melodies she is singing. She chisels the words to perfection, without diluting their meaning with too much mannerism; her breath is steady; she masters the effects she calculates with science, her nuances are chosen, her colors are subtle, and the singing line she imposes on herself never ceases to shine. She is a great singer, endowed with a most uncommon artistic awareness and dazzling artistic results.

Would you define yourself as a feminist?

*National Anthem of France.

Obviously, I'm committed to defending the equal rights—and responsibilities—of women as well as those my own. Equality in treatment and consideration, *and equal indifference with respect to sex.* I am grateful to all the "feminists" who have fought throughout history to make it possible for me, today, to live as I choose, without being disgraced or, worse, burned alive—and undoubtedly would have been for my rebellious spirit, my independence, and what about my dealings with wolves and the natural world? But while I cherish the right to be different—to choose my own destiny and way of life—I also cherish the right to be *indifferent.* In the name of this I ask that we finally stop judging women's work by this criterion, as we do too often today, and I would even say more and more often, as if it were the only important criterion for evaluating the work. A few years ago, I was recruited by Amnesty International to campaign on the terrible issue of abused women, and for once, I agreed to take part in a joint action. I did so because it is undeniable and repugnant that women around the world continue to suffer from oppression by men, physical and moral violence, and discrimination of all kinds. The weakest children are also the victims of brutality. However, I have my doubts about the effectiveness of voluntary segregation and about asking women to express themselves primarily on the basis of their gender. Doesn't this mean recognizing that their artistic production—cinematography, for example—is its own genre? Not to say a subgenre? Is Jane Campion a great director, yes or no? I always smile when blind recordings of the same piano piece are submitted to several critics. I've never heard any of them guess whether the pianist was a man or a woman, and that's very fortunate—the point of the exercise was to establish a preference among the selected pieces. Because I'm in favor of equal treatment for men and women, I protest against what I see as a sterile, pernicious and liberticidal process.

I'm sure I'm a feminist when I see this unequal treatment, which betrays a deep-seated sense of condescension and superiority among many people. The proof is in the use of first names. Have you noticed in newspaper articles, the almost systematic use of first names when the person being referred to is a woman? Never when it's a man? They use Martha to refer to Argerich; would you read Ivo for Pogorelić or Alfred for Brendel? It's a small liberty, a familiarity that speaks volumes about the inequality of esteem, sometimes unconscious, between male and female artists. The difference in treatment certainly has very deep roots. Let's take the example of Clara Schumann, an exceptional virtuoso and promising composer. Why did she one day stop all creative activity? And Alma Mahler? Why was she overshadowed by her husband? Why did Fanny Mendelssohn, first bullied by her father and then by her brother Felix, for bid herself to compose? The examples are legion. Why did these women of such character accept being silenced? I have an answer: Men know that in areas where they've established a monopoly, with the exception of our time, they can be surpassed by certain women. Not all—geniuses are rare in both sexes. And from that point, women can escape them, escape their domination, their constraints, and if not, truly inspire other women by setting a "bad" example. So they did not permit them to express themselves. The most remarkable individuals did this: Mahler or Mendelssohn. Rimbaud had already pointed this out: "When the infinite servitude of women shall have ended, when she will be able to live by and for herself, then man, hitherto abominable, having given her her freedom, she too will be a poet. Woman will discover the unknown."

You know that the musicologist Viviane Wascherbüsch, who's also a composer and violinist, wrote a study about the reactions you've inspired. It was published in the book *La musique a-t-elle un genre?** edited by Mélanie Traversier and Alban Ramaut (Éditions de la Sorbonne). In her text, she shows how the media has often presented a distorted image of you.

Yes, there's no doubt about it, and you have got to get over it. It's an old story, you might say. Wasn't it Maurice Blanchot who wrote about the siren song in the Ulysses legend: "There has always been an ignoble effort on the part of men to discredit Sirens by flatly accusing them of lying: liars when they sang, deceitful when they sighed, fictitious when approached; non-existent in short, a puerile non-existence that Ulysses is able to exterminate by simply using his common sense?" He goes on to describe them as ". . . beautiful girls, real and worthy of their promise, so they could disappear into the truth and depth of their song." It's important to persevere in the uniqueness of our being and to trust in the resources of our powers.

I'd like to quote a text you wrote:

> *"Why do we play? Why do we write? Why do we fight? To reach as many people as possible? I don't think so. It's rather the opposite:*

**Does Music Have a Gender?*

to touch those who, like you, like me, are driven by a hunger, a thirst that nothing can satisfy. Art, in general, is no different from hunger or thirst—it's a vital need, an urgent necessity: it's the place where we can be reborn. Suffice it to say that if we live without art, without the many opportunities and secret joys it offers—not to mention the dangers it poses—we condemn ourselves to living beside ourselves. We miss the essence of that other life: our inner life, our personal citadel, against which no one can do anything."

Doesn't this text also say something about your feminine specificity, your desire to build bridges?

Probably. Women are more naturally placed than men in a state of trust that can be described as absolute, which is why they are so often its victims. The philosopher René Girard summed up the situation beautifully: "What we men have all inherited from Adam is not only his desire, but the perverse taste of blaming women for it, of making our companions scapegoats"—and at the same time making them the door to their salvation. An important thinker, Paul Evdokimov, wrote this:

> Man the warrior and technician dehumanizes the world, while the prayerful woman humanizes it as a mother who watches over every human form as if it were her own child. Today, in the face of the tragedy of the Third World, in the face of materialism, pornography, drugs and all the elements of decay, it is the woman who is predestined to say "No!" To stop man on the brink of the abyss, and to show him his true vocation.

As far as I can see, all over the world, women give themselves to men because they love them, and this love doesn't keep them away from life; on the contrary, it brings them closer to it. They are the great mediators; that's their mission, not to model themselves on the worst copy of masculinity. Women make the world and weave the link between it and men. Without this link, it won't even be the alternative "adapt or die," it will be the prophecy of the Apocalypse:* "In those days men will seek death and will not find it; they will desire to die, and death will flee from them."

---

*Revelation 9:6.

10

ECOFEMINISM

What do you think about the feminism of today?

Although the subject interests me, I am not a historian of the movement. I repeat: I am grateful to the women who preceded me in history for fighting to put an end to all forms and excesses of patriarchy. I also know that the word *feminism* encompasses different movements that have responded to the constraints and challenges affecting them in each era. Nevertheless, a political trend that emerged in the middle of the last century strikes me as a historical turning point: The class struggle was replaced by the war between the sexes, under the guise, at least initially, of equality between them, only to end up, logically enough, in a war of all against all, in which each defends, in effect, its superiority: men against women, women against men. Now, nothing enchants me more than harmony in music and between individuals. However, there is a feminist movement that has caught my attention, I think it's called ecofeminism. It was a French woman, Françoise d'Eaubonne, who introduced the name in 1974. She was alarmed by the damage that human activity was inflicting on nature, and the succession of disasters that followed one another in that decade and the years that followed—Three Mile Island in the United States, Seveso in Italy, Bhopal in India, Greenham Common in England—highlight her analyses. She became particularly popular in the 1980s, and I remember my mother discussing the subject with friends. The close connection she made between ecological and feminist issues seems to me well founded and relevant. Later, the pacifist movements joined in, and I'm happy to see that more and more women are joining their ranks. Feminist ecologists haven't limited their analysis of phenomena affecting the planet solely to issues of the resource depletion, vanishing species, and biodiversity loss.

They extend their observations to the ways in which the planet is exploited by what they call "the male system." I was struck by the subtlety of many of their observations. And without endorsing their radicalism, and even less their excesses, especially the hatred of "males" by some, I can only agree with what they highlight. For example, they have presented farmers from all over the world with the latest studies on soil management techniques—the art of tilling the soil. It has been proven that in order to get a good harvest without damaging the soil or compromising its richness, shallow plowing is required. Well, nobody listened to them. There's this need to dig deep with the harrow to plow layers that should remain virgin—I use the word advisedly; what these feminists have proposed is a very close connection between the oppression of women and the oppression of nature, both victims of rape. This movement asserts, and I quote, that "understanding the state of these connections is indispensable to any attempt to adequately grasp the oppression of women as well as that of nature." Theorists in this movement see direct links between patriarchal violence against women and men's violence against nature and people. They condemn the direct links between industrial and military aggression against the environment and physical aggression against women. Some go even farther by linking the violence of war and environmental destruction to the violence of rape. Again, there are extremely radical schools of this branch of feminism. But I'm interested in many of their theories, especially those that extend this point of view into a spiritual dimension emphasizing the close relationship of the feminine to nature and the cosmos. They assume that women are much more inclined to protect nature, if only to ensure the future and comfort of their children. In their view, the struggle for ecology can only be waged through the struggle for feminism, and vice versa. They link the two with a permanent glue, while giving priority to the struggle for the planet. They consider it sterile to confine the struggle for women to a sphere that concerns only themselves. And it is undeniable that violence against women is only one aspect of the violence for which men—and women—are responsible, and that we must go to the root of this evil and fight it with means other than coercion, because, as we know, prison doesn't eradicate crime.

What also interested me when I heard about this movement was its policy of forming alliances with women of the Third World who are generally very receptive to issues related to the preservation of the planet. They live closely with nature and witness the depletion of resources and the attacks on biodiversity because they have their hands in the dirt as farmers. And it's also because they take care of children and livestock. They are the protectors of seeds and water purity; they are the guarantors of our future.

Did you get a chance to meet these women?

During my trip to the center of the United States, which I drove through at the time of the pandemic because most of the airports were closed, I met a young woman named Rosie. She was a Cheyenne descendant of one of the rare survivors of the Sand Creek Massacre. She invited me to meet her family. She told me about a woman she greatly admired, who had just died from the breast cancer she had fought for years. She showed me her picture. A woman in her sixties, her hair woven with silver, sleek and beautiful. Her gaze was haughty, but without contempt or condescension. She could have been Sitting Bull's daughter. Her real name was Tamakawastewin. Her legal name was LaDonna Brave Bull Allard. A Lakota. Her people called her "the mother of water." This woman had initiated and led the protest movement against the construction of an oil pipeline* that would cut through the land of Iowa farmers and the ancestral lands of her tribe, destroying their burial ground and potentially contaminating the reservation's groundwater.

Throughout her medical treatment, and until to her death, she never backed down, despite the harassment and threats she faced. My friend showed me the film of her protests in front of the Indian tribes she had called to her aid blocking the bulldozers on the construction site. They had all come, some even from Brazil, and set up their teepees on the lands that had been theirs since the dawn of time. Farmers had come to join the protests. Intellectuals and actors had joined this cause that affected everyone—a leak of the oil pipeline would contaminate

*Dakota Access Pipeline.

the entire water table for hundreds of miles. She had persuaded hundreds of women with her speech by reminding them that water was a woman, and that thanks to water, women could give birth and feed their families, and that plants, animals, and trees could grow. My young friend Rosie had gone to join these people. The atmosphere that LaDonna had created there had inspired her. The time of resistance in the growing teepee village had been a wonderful time of understanding and sharing. Many young ecological activists had come to join them. They wanted to learn how to set up a teepee and sleep in it, then learn about the "native" art they still practice of living as close to nature as possible, without electricity, in religious respect for the elements—earth, water and fire. My young friend then explained to me how the Indians have never stopped passing on to their children the science of medicinal plants, the art of fire, and the art of listening to the sky. LaDonna had told them of the four days that the Indians devote to water every year, their ablutions, their baths, their sacred ceremonies, and the fasting they impose on themselves. She reminded them of their culture's principle of treating life with sacred respect and nature with immense gratitude, without stealing from her what they do not really need, and always looking for ways to return the gifts she bestowed on humanity. Soon, many of these young Americans, farmers, and urban dwellers began to call LaDonna "Mama." Unfortunately, in the end, the Energy Transfer Partners won the battle. The oil pipeline is currently in operation.

But with all the strength of gentleness, and the power of a true word, she convinced thousands of young people to join in a daily struggle, and taught them that it begins very humbly. After the dismantling of the Standing Rock teepee village LaDonna solemnly asked them to continue to stand watch:

> Each of us has to make this decision: to clean the environment, our rivers, our creeks, our oceans. . . . We can change the world step by step. In twenty years you will see how the whole world has become "eco," and that ecology makes jobs, wealth, and most importantly, life.

LaDonna opened the eyes of Native Americans, North and South. They had pledged to leave their reservations behind, no pun intended, and realized that their way of life and culture was the only effective, rational, and peaceful response to the global energy crisis and, by extension, to dramatic climate change. Finally, my young friend had shared a most disturbing fact with me. A Lakota medicine man had made a prophecy a long time ago: one day, a black snake would emerge on their sacred lands. It would be a sign of the rebirth of the Oceti Sakowin, the Sioux people. Coincidentally, the black snake was the name that the Native Americans had spontaneously given to the oil pipeline. And this "seventh generation," which, according to this shaman's prophecy, would restore life to the Sioux nation, was the generation of my friend.

Were you convinced—if not to say converted yourself—by these words about the new relationship to be established with nature and the way in which man occupies the planet?

At first I was very disturbed by my meeting with Rosie. By the random chance that had led me to this young woman. Such an unlikely meeting! Had it not been for the lockdown in place then, our paths would have never crossed. Another coincidence was this young woman telling me about the struggle of an entire population for water, while barely three years earlier, I had personally decided to extend my struggle for ecology to this vital element, to express the source of inspiration it has been for art and music. It's for this reason—to establish correspondences and show the connection between all things, between nature and art—that I recorded on the same record, called *Water,* the compositions of Berio, Takemitsu, Fauré, Ravel, Albéniz, Liszt, Janáček, and Debussy, all inspired by water. Aquatic sorrow in Berio, rain in Takemitsu, dancing waters in the works of Fauré and Ravel, sensual waves in Albéniz, epicurean spurting from Liszt, mist in Janáček, and gravity with Debussy's *Sunken Cathedral.* Through the timbre, the arpeggios, the impression of undulation and constant movement . . . this is water music. But the poetic dimension goes beyond that. Torrents, clouds, fog: It's an epiphany of water in all its states. In life as in water, water is a redemptive element of healing and survival that possesses something profoundly spiritual. I interspersed these compositions with pieces by British composer Nitin Sawhney, a pioneer of the underground electronic music scene. I did this to emphasize the fluidity of music, the flow from one school to another, from one genre to another, and to show that it's not always wise to put music in an airtight jar. At a time of international exchange, of culinary, social and cultural mixing, which is so beneficial to our understanding of others, should culture and its expressions, on the contrary, be specialized to such an extreme, at the risk of becoming hardened and paralyzed? Water, so threatened in its purity, its abundance and its distribution in the world, seems to me to have few defenders better than musicians, for the beauty with which they make us hear and see it. To listen to water is to listen to nature. That is why this coincidence between the message of *Water* and the struggle waged by LaDonna disturbed me.

Today, more than six-hundred-and-sixty-million people around the world struggle every day to obtain safe drinking water. Unclean water kills a child every ninety seconds. Not to mention industrial pollution. It's the most pressing humanitarian crisis of our century. So, to answer your question, yes, I was convinced of the validity of this Indian struggle long before I heard of it. In fact, I'm even angry at myself for missing this event—the occupation of Standing Rock. And I hope with all my heart that the prediction of the Lakota shaman, that my friend told me about, will come true.

Had you reached out to Indians before this encounter? You have told us that you were interested in shamans and their relationship with the elements.

I fell in love with the world of the "Natives" the day I discovered the music albums of a photographer named Edward Curtis. And I can't forget the first time I had all the free time to do so, in the hushed halls of the Morgan Library on Madison Avenue. I'd had the privilege of looking first at his photographs, after I'd left Tallahassee, when I'd moved to New York and dreamed of returning to Alawa. I had entered this vast building, which resembles one of those Gothic castles still admired in the English countryside. The library is dizzying, as tall as a cathedral. I can still see the huge tomes bound in red leather with gold highlights and remember the emotion that gripped me as these portraits passed by, page after page. Some posed in front of large, stretched-out sheets, others on the spot, and one could feel, in the dissolution of the horizon in the background, the immensity, the emptiness, the boundless plains characteristic of the American space. The sharp gaze of the models was directed toward the distant, the most distant horizon; what this camera, in front of which they had agreed to pose, foretold for them was their future, their survival. I looked at these photographs with the feeling of crossing from one abyss to another. These imperiously present faces had brought me to the threshold of another world, endowed with other suns, and yes, I told myself at the time that Eden must have resembled these spaces in a unique way. How Adam and Eve, if they had to cover their bodies, would resemble these silhouettes, a little lost in their embroidered skin garments, decorated with pearls, feathers, and shells.

After discovering Curtis's pictures, I wanted to know more about the life of this meticulous and enthusiastic photographer, whose images revealed all the affection, respect, and even tenderness he felt for the Indians. The Indians returned the favor, quickly realizing that under the cruel and relentless wave of new settlers arriving every day, their essentially oral culture—or one that was barely written in ideograms on fragile, perishable birch bark—had a chance to be preserved, fixed, and recognized thanks to Curtis's photographic work. The possibility of continuing to exist when they themselves were gone, when their invaders, and with them Roosevelt, their President were gone. "He became an Indian, he lived and spoke Indian; he was a kind of Great White Brother. He spent the best years of his life, like the renegades of old, among the Indians," a journalist—whose name I cannot recall—wrote about Edward Curtis, and as I read this, I thought how much I would like someone to say the same thing about me one day: "She became music (or a wolf). She lived and spoke music; she was a kind human (or wolf) Great Sister."

I was fascinated by his life—that of an adventurer consumed by his passion, who found meaning and purpose in his art. Edward Curtis who had built his first camera at the age of twelve, and who had moved heaven and earth to apprentice with a photographer in St. Paul. When his family decided to move to Seattle in the far northwest, he decided to open his first photography studio. His work was so meticulous, so perfect, his knowledge of camera technique so infallible, that when Edward Henry Harriman, the famous billionaire railroad builder, decided to hire a team of scientists to explore the Pacific coast from Seattle to the Alaskan frontier, he asked Curtis to close his shop and join the expedition. Edward Curtis's many wanderings, following in his preacher father's footsteps as he set out by mule, foot, or canoe to spread the gospel in uncharted lands, were undoubtedly something that the adult he had become missed. He accepted without hesitation. This journey revealed to him his vocation: ethnology. Fascinated by the life and culture of the Indians he met during this expedition, he decided to study the life and customs of other tribes. First it was the Plains Indians—the tribes of the great flat grassy plains I was soon to cross—nomads who, in the 1880s, were trying to continue to live hunting buffalo.

In order to apply a completely scientific method to his photography and recording, Curtis took an anthropologist with him on his travels. From that day on, he never stopped trying to capture what remained of the customs, celebrations, habitat, and dress of the Sioux and Cheyenne, the Comanche and Apache, and all the other tribes whose ties to the cosmos that surrounded them, their relationships with the spirit of the elements, their dances and ceremonies, he also noted. John Pierpont Morgan, a New York billionaire who had been enchanted by his first photographs, generously financed the mission, which was soon supported by President Roosevelt. It was again Morgan who took charge of publishing the twenty volumes of Curtis's collected works. Among the fifty thousand photographs he had taken over the years, just two thousand five hundred pictures were kept for the North American Indian edition.

What did you learn from these photographic works?

They aroused my curiosity about a culture to which I felt so instinctively close. I was already toying with the idea of opening a center to collect wolves and reintroduce them into the wild as part of the SSP (Species Survival Plan) program. There's no escaping clichés and associations. I associated wolves with Jack London, *White Fang,* and the Far North but also, of course, with those people who had adapted so well. For a long time, these people were considered inferior, and it was imagined that women had an even more inferior role to play. I've since learned how wrong that was. As I became more interested in Edward Curtis's work, I discovered that in the 1880s the American ethnologist Alice Fletcher, who was also a suffragette, had recently revealed to Americans that Sioux women had the right to divorce, and that they owned their land, voted in tribal councils, and controlled their fertility—all rights unknown to American women. Perhaps this is why Indian women were objectified with such disdain by colonists, lumberjacks, gold seekers, preachers, and sectarian Mormons. They called them "squaws." Now, this term designates a second-class human being and is the equivalent of the word "whore." That's how much the white world valued Indian women. It shows the racism and misogyny of a term as contemptuous and demeaning as "nigger" or "négresse."

And yet it was they who, then as now, tirelessly maintained the hearth of the Indian Great Spirit, for they were and are the ones who transmit the precepts of shamanism and its liturgies. "The Sioux religion is the only one in the world taught by a woman and intended for men," said Lakota Chief Archie Fire Lame Deer when he met with the Pope and the Dalai Lama. In the legends of this people, it was White Buffalo Calf Woman who taught the Sioux how to pray. She taught them how to sing the precious intonations that allowed them to join the concert of birds and trees. She taught them how to fill the pipe and the sacred gestures that would project its purifying, peace-giving smoke to the heavens, to the depths of the earth, and far into the four directions. When calling upon Wakan Tanka—the Great Spirit or the Great Mystery—the White Buffalo Woman, their Spiritual Mother, told her people: With this holy pipe you will walk like a living prayer. With your feet resting upon the earth and the pipe stem reaching into the sky, your body forms a living bridge between the Sacred Beneath and the Sacred Above. Wakan Tanka smiles upon us, because now we are as one: earth, sky, all living things, the two-legged, the four-legged, the winged ones, the trees, the grasses. Together with the people, they are all related, one family. The pipe holds them all together.

These women, like LaDonna, made it clear that there can be

no love without ecology. They spread the core of their beliefs: Everything that walks, flies, breathes, grows, even air, stone, water and wind, has an immortal spirit. There's something sacred in everything, and at bottom, everything is one. All beings are connected. The resistance of Indian women, no longer armed but intellectual, cultural, and memorialized, has kept their people from being completely crushed under the weight of the modern world. In past centuries they were spiritual initiators, shamans, negotiators, and healers. Much freer and more respected than their European counterparts, they played an important role in the tribes and enjoyed equal rights with men. So much so that in the late nineteenth century they even influenced the American suffragette movement, which at the instigation of Alice Fletcher had come to study their way of life and social organization.

And so, a few miles from Lincoln, in the town of Omaha, where she was born in the mid-nineteenth century, they could have met a young Native American woman who had studied medicine, passed her exams and earned her degree, and then returned to practice her art on her tribe's reservation, enriching her science with the knowledge of her culture. Her name was Susan La Flesche Picotte. Farther north, in Lakota territory, there was also Zitkala-Sa—which means "Red Bird"—whose name was changed to Gertrude Simmons Bonnin by the institution that admitted her, as required by law. After learning to play the violin, she composed the first Native American opera, *The Sun Dance.* Then she embarked on another great mission: to collect the legends of her tribe, to fight for her people, to shed light on the injustices perpetrated against them. And how could we forget Pocahontas, or La Malinche and Sacagawea, less famous but still inseparable from the great episodes of Indian history? William Faulkner warned: "If you don't care about Indians, you don't understand anything about America."* Today their names are LaDonna, of course, Elizabeth Cook-Lynn, Janet McCloud—whose Indian name "Yet-Sit-Blue" means "The Woman Who Speaks"—Luci Tapahonso, or Mona Susan Power. They are novelists, artists and spokeswomen for their people, or civil rights or environmental lawyers. Whether they are one hundred percent Native American or mixed race, they are always at the forefront of the fight against oblivion, and for the protection of the planet and its ecosystem. I'm passionate about their story because the story of the American Indians is one of the great myths of humanity, because their spirituality, their vision of the world and the cosmos are today the only guarantees for a better future, and because where we try to crush them, we crush an ecological awakening, and finally because, as the Cheyenne proverb says: "A nation is not conquered until the hearts of its women are on the ground.

It's striking that, as a pianist, you've been confronted on several occasions with history in the making, in its most political dimension. I'm thinking, for example, of the concert you gave with Christoph Eschenbach and the Orchestre de Paris at the Proms on the evening of September 11, 2001.

I have a terrifyingly precise and physical memory of what we were doing the minute we found out what had happened in New York. I was in London. I had returned to the hotel after a working ses-

*Although sometimes attributed to Faulkner, the exact source of this quote is unknown.

sion at the Royal Albert Hall and asked that no one disturb me. The television was suddenly turned on with no sound. I saw these horrible images and wondered if it was a movie or reality. It was only when I listened to the message that the hotel receptionist had left for all the guests that I understood what happened. An hour later, we were all back together. Should we play that night? The question arose as much for the safety of the spectators as for reasons of appropriateness. The Proms organizers and the orchestra's management then made the decision we'd been clamoring for, despite the difficulty of keeping a level head: we'd play. To my surprise, the hall was packed; no one had backed out. And the audience carried us. I would never have believed it possible to play Beethoven's work so . . . back to its vital necessity. It was as if we supported each other. It was then that I understood, as never before, what an ensemble is, and the power of a pain that seeks its solace and finds its rhythm in spite of the discord that life offers.

In a different key, this experience was repeated in 2015, when I shared another historic moment, again with the Orchestre de Paris, at the invitation of Laurent Bayle, namely the inauguration of the Paris Philharmonic under the direction of Paavo Järvi. This was the first time the hall had been used, but more importantly, it was the first cultural event after the attacks of January 7th* that cost so many innocent lives, as well as the attacks against the journalists and the offices of *Charlie Hebdo*, and against the customers of the Hyper Cacher at the Porte de Vincennes, on January 9th. On January 14th, we found ourselves playing in front of some of France's leading political figures. The atmosphere was more than tense. What should have

*Attack on satirical newspaper *Charlie Hebdo*.

been a celebration could not be. And just like in London, we didn't hesitate. It was important to not only reiterate our solidarity with the innocent lives sacrificed, but also show how music, and all that it underpins, must be an answer, not in the rise to extremes, nor in a politics of repeated violence, but in the alternative of a demand for beauty and contemplation—that beauty that does not deny tragedy, but offers it a counterweight, a resilience. After the concert I spoke with President Hollande. But my thoughts kept straying back to the dead. To all those whose lives were brutally, absurdly, and unjustly cut short, and who remind us that life deserves to be lived as joyously as possible.

11

SPIRITUAL MOTHERHOOD

You don't hesitate to call yourself a witch, or even a fairy. In fact, you've told me what epitaph you'd like to see carved on your tombstone. Do you see these definitions in the vein of the ecofeminism you've just described?

As for the epitaph, I may change it tomorrow. Or I'll only demand it if I'm burned at the stake. Something that's not impossible—violence doesn't stop increasing in the world, and that against women follows the same rising curve. In answer to your question, for a long time I felt an affinity with those who were called witches in the past. I discovered their history by studying the history of wolves, and learned about the origins of the persecution to which they were subjected. I became all the more interested because the same predatory violence was used against wolves as against women. The author Clarissa Pinkola Estés wrote that the history of wolves bears strange similarities to that of women, both in passion and toil. And it's true that wolves and women share certain psychic traits: heightened senses, playful spirit, and an extreme capacity for devotion. Women were accused of witchcraft when they assumed the power of miracle workers, when they shared their knowledge of herbal medicine, when they cured and healed with their balms, ointments, and decoctions made after gathering wild herbs. They escaped the authority and control of fathers and husbands. They were immediately punished for the power that their primitive, wild, essential relationship with nature revealed to them. We wanted to crush their memory of the Garden, from which beauty and loss sometimes awaken strange memories and powerful intuitions. Some were burned, others banished. In still others, when they run in the moonlight, their shadow stretches and shakes itself like that of a she-wolf. They are the ones who laugh and love without restraint, who give birth and create, who rejoice in their shapes and the hot blood that flows from their bodies, and who instinctively know the virtues of every herb and which fruits hold poison. They are the women revered by Native Americans in the north. They are the ones that the *cantadoras** of South America sing and invoke as "the woman who lives at the end of time" or "the woman who lives at the edge of the world." This woman, this she-wolf, is always the friend and mother of those who are lost and those who need to know, and who have a mystery to solve, of those who wander in the desert or in the forest, looking for an answer, a sign, a hope. So yes, I'm not averse to associating myself with her. Proust spoke of the "*the face of this great poet* who is essentially one, since the beginning of the world,

*Women who sing and compose songs in traditional Colombian music.

whose intermittent life, [is] as long as that of humanity." We could repeat the same vision of these women and mothers. We would see that since the dawn of time, there has been only one woman, always different, always generous, who showers us all with every shade of her unique talent—love.

The many movements that claim to be either witchcraft or shamanism don't surprise me. What I see in them is a desire to return to our roots, a dream of mastering the future of the planet, and a re-appropriation of our own strengths. I like them because they connect women to the idea of the sacred feminine, which is also the essence of our planet, Earth. Women have an intuition for the common good and a concern for the future, which they want to be able to prepare for the happiness of their children. Anita Diamant's 1997 international bestseller, *The Red Tent,* was an early revelation of this aspiration. The novel tells the story of Dinah, a biblical character who shares secrets and rites with the other women of her tribe, in a scarlet tent, a place forbidden to men. It is, in fact, an ode to femininity.

Going back to the question of feminism, do you feel that you were treated differently when you were a student than you were later with your agents or in organizing your concerts?

No matter where you come from, if you look a little closer, you'll find everything human nature is capable of, the best and the worst. The world of classical music is no different. Is it also sexist? It's inevitable. If there's sexism in Hollywood, imagine it in classical music! But there are more and more women in the industry, and that helps to shake things up. So I too have noticed a difference in treatment compared to my colleagues, and this has been true throughout my studies. It was subtle, just a few details at the beginning of my career. Patronizing attitudes. Different compensations. A slight tendency to be intimate. The use of only my first name in articles, which I've condemned. But on the one hand, I know how to stand up for myself. On the other hand, I don't dwell on these incidents. The battle is elsewhere. When I was still a child, had the good fortune to receive masterful advice from Pierre Barbizet: "Don't try to be the best, try to be unique." Each individual is unique; individual means indivisible. His or her destiny is to develop that part of him or herself that makes him or her incomparable, unclassifiable, neither man nor woman, neither black nor white, neither blond nor brown, neither old nor young. Let's put an end to these classifications, unworthy of humanism and hardly worthy of a zoologist. What counts is the soul of each being, not its sex. It's his ability to create himself, to create, and to produce beauty. It's up to women to assert themselves, each according to her talents, even if the obstacles are more numerous than for men, I don't deny it, instead of getting lost in hopeless victimization. Today there are laws, lawyers, judges, and punishments. Let them act so that these laws are applied to those who deserve to be denounced, judged, and condemned if they are guilty. But I sense a danger for women if they allow themselves to be locked into chronic victimization by this system of systematic over-legalization and accept the reduction of their identities to their sexual relations, the #MeToo version, and with them the scope of their struggles. The world can only be saved and reformed from above. I'm thinking of Empress Theodora, Justinian's wife, who ruled at his side and implemented a series of reforms in favor of women's rights. All art and the entire civilization were renewed, as in Ravenna, by the new meaning given to woman then by the heart and life. It's up to each era to create its own Theodora, and for each of us to want to be her. Nor do I forget that women initiated the great revitalization of societies when they began to go under. This is the vocation of the saint, of the witch and of the fairy, the vocation of woman: birth. Rebirth.

You don't have a child yourself. You have often talked about adopting one. Does that mean you don't want one yourself? That you prefer what some call spiritual motherhood, or what the feminist Marie-Jo Bonnet calls "symbolic motherhood"? I'll quote her:

> *Symbolic motherhood has always existed. It gives birth to ideas, art works, books, the inner child; it takes care of others and helps them to grow. It heals souls. Patriarchal culture knows this, and it has restricted this symbolic motherhood to redemptive and merciful virgins, maintaining the separation between the body (maternal) and the spirit (divine). This explains why symbolic motherhood is so little known. While it was thought in the 1970s that women's newfound access to control over their fertility would finally allow them to freely enjoy motherhood, we were disillusioned. Artificial reproduction techniques regained control over women's bodies, reactivated the fear of sterility and stigmatized women who didn't have children. From cults to mother goddesses to Socratic maieutics, from Thérèse d'Avila and Jeanne Guyon to the Mother of Auroville and Niki de Saint Phalle to ecofeminism and shamans, it's important to open the*

> *debate by showing that symbolic motherhood is part of the universal experience. It is both an alternative to compulsory motherhood and a means of expressing one's creative impulse, whether mystical, artistic or healing.*

That's the perfect example of a question that is never asked of an artist who is a man. But I can answer it. For a long time I believed that the earth was overpopulated, which is true, but it was also a way to defend myself against the social pressure that compels women to have children. In any case, we must always be careful to distinguish between the two: One can be a parent without being a mother. A genetrix* is the biological fact. A mother is the spiritual fact, and that's the only one that counts. But even without a child, you can be a mother in spirit. When I'm playing or taking care of the animals, I'm trying to give birth to each one of them. Starting with myself, because you can only be a mother if you become your own mother. Last but not least, I was interested in all the children I wanted to bring to the Wolf Conservation Center, especially handicapped children, a word whose etymology I liked to imagine. Handicapped: "hand to the head."† A hand that emphasizes pain or the difference from others. No doubt that's why I preferred them to all the other visitors, and I see the word handicap as similar to "invalid," something you would say of a train ticket or broken washing machine. At the Wolf Conservation Center, all the young visitors look the same to the wolves: They are children. In front of these children who are autistic or have lost the use

---

*Female progenitor.

†Etymology of this word suggests it is more akin to "hand in cap" which has a slightly different connotation.

of their legs, the pack doesn't change their behavior in any way. Their games, their loves, their glances, or their runs form the alphabet of a language that dispenses with words or judgments. The mother who feeds her cubs is a universal mother. She continues to frolic with them in the snow, without changing her facial expressions—no signs of pity, or compassion, or embarrassment, or any false, noisy expressions of empathy. Here are these children, usually sheltered from the world by the thick, if not truly suffocating insulation of hospital and institutional care, with their feet in the snow or mud, their noses in the blizzard or smelling the scents of spring, not simply in contact with nature, but in the heart of what nature has to offer that is most authentic and most radically vital: wolves. This spectacle is constructive for all of them, I think, because it puts them in touch with that part of themselves that is the instinct for life, even for survival. The sense of wonder is there, and the dialogue is established with what's essential: the profound joy of being in the world, even when you are different.

Finally, getting back to that question of my own children, in addition to the question every woman asks before bringing a child into the world: "Can I impose this world on an innocent being?" There is the life of a concert musician, which leaves little time for a home life, for family life, for children that need a mother's presence and attention. I don't know if as a child I would have liked my mother to not be there when I came home from school. I was privileged that her job allowed her to be there. Have you seen Ingmar Bergman's film, *Autumn Sonata*? And do you know many children of artists who wouldn't have felt the same about their mother as Eva does about Charlotte, a concert performer, who she blames for sacrificing her for her career?

Be that as it may there is also an . . . inequality between men and women in the artistic domain. If a female performer has children, she will be scolded—by her husband, her children, those around her—for not putting them before her career. If she doesn't have any, no one will know of her sacrifice—and it is a sacrifice. And it's not always a choice. There are diseases that can prevent pregnancy. It's now fashionable to give a voice to women who don't have maternal feelings for their children, who are far more numerous than you might think. Who is going to spare a thought for the torment of a woman who hasn't had a child, even if she wanted to?

You have a beauty that our contemporaries have found striking. Ingmar Bergman himself, who filmed femininity so powerfully, asked to meet you and planned to film you. I remember a trip we took to Sweden when you were unable to accept his invitation to visit him at his home on the island, of Fårö, in the Baltic Sea.

Has your physical appearance been a blessing or a curse? We are familiar with the observation by the actress Louise Brooks: "I always thought that my beauty was a calamity. It's only today that I realized that my beauty was a blessing. It's the fact that I didn't know how to take advantage of it that was a calamity." There's also the apt line from one of Alfred de Musset's plays:

> *You think I'm pretty, I suppose, and it amuses you to tell me so. Well, what's next? What does that prove? Is it a reason for me to like you? I suppose if someone likes me, it's not because I'm pretty. What's in it for him? What a great way to make someone love you,*

> *to stand in front of a woman with a pince-nez, looking at her from head to toe, like a doll on a shelf, and very pleasantly telling her, 'Madame, I find you charming!' Throw in a few insipid phrases, a waltz, and a bouquet, and you've got something called courtship. How can a man of spirit fall for such nonsense? It infuriates me when I think about it.*

During an interview one day, I was asked what I would change about myself if I could. I spontaneously replied: "The way other people look at me." However, I don't think that beauty—physical beauty—is a curse. It is only if you let it rule you, if you become its slave. I didn't bear mine that way, nor did I see it as a sign of superiority. Professionally, it may have helped me—it is hard to wonder if my career or decisions would have been different with a different face. It also hurt me. I've often heard the cliché "too pretty to play well." Many times I've been judged by the eyes instead of the ears, and I deplore that. Would anyone say that a man is . . . too handsome? When I'm at the piano, there's no room for cheating; I put myself on the line. Music demands the nakedness of the whole soul. But people still want to believe that a woman can't be talented on her own, as if everything depended on her looks. This prejudice, which is considered absurd, is always perpetrated by men who are afraid of women.

Finally, my rebellious, undisciplined nature and my turbulent childhood shielded me from narcissistic temptations from a very early age. I've never given it much importance. Fortunately, my lifestyle protects me from the kind of harassment that, unfortunately, affects far too many women. When I'm not on tour, I live in the middle of nowhere, deep in the woods, and often in solitude. But I felt this sexual pressure in my teens, exploring the streets of Paris between classes at the conservatory. I'd held onto the habit, perhaps a provincial one, of looking people straight in the eye when I passed them. When I was fifteen, I discovered the peculiar way some men look at women—and their terrible smiles, because they held no kindness or gentleness, and because they glisten with violence unheard of for a girl of that age. The look of lust has a thousand variations. Some are mocking, some more shy—but with something obscene underneath. I have met eyes lit up by a lecherous gleam. Glances of infinite melancholy—those of men who deny themselves the forbidden fruit yet dream of tasting it and are poisoned daily by the venom of their desire. But for me, as for all the girls in the world, there was something chilling about the inspection of which I was the object and the gleam of those eyes staring at me, because they exuded a primal, barbaric essence, a pure, nuclear violence, a glimpse of enormous, voracious black forces that had nothing to do with those that I witnessed in nature, and which I respected. Over the years, I've learned to remain impervious to those stares. Not that I have rejected this power to disturb others, nor have I completely rejected any narcissistic temptation. It's just that when I discovered it, I also realized I had no control over it. I was willing to be incendiary, but only at the time and place of my choosing, certainly not because of my appearance or the effect of my smile, nor because of my eyes. To ignite the fire of passion, yes, but for my musical visions, my ideas about the world, my union with the piano, which used to make me regret the lack of a Sagittarius half-man half-piano or a mermaid with a body of strings and rippling chords in fabulous bestiaries or musical mythologies.

To extinguish the stares of the men I passed by in the street as I roamed about, I learned to give an almost athletic determination to the way I walked. Nothing is worse than nonchalance, that singular wandering stride, to trigger misunderstandings and ambiguities. And then, very quickly, I stopped looking at the people and if by chance I still happened to encounter certain looks, they no longer reached me or touched me in any way. Later, when I embarked on an international career, people were often taken aback by my appearance, or rather the combination of my appearance and my professional background, which seemed unimaginable to many. The "Be pretty and keep quiet" that any woman inspires at first sight was ruined by my concerts, this last element contradicted by my confessed, active passion for a pack of wolves . . . How do I fit all these puzzle pieces together?

Writing three books didn't make it any easier, although I've pretty much explained it. A pianist (hence she's "pure"), a classical musician (hence she has an "intellect"), launched on an international career (hence financially independent and free to move about) and writing. So far, so good. But "living with wolves" (an image that generates fantasies of sexual prowess); then all kinds of misunderstandings arise!

You invoked the figure of Theodora and said that this role model should be an inspiration to women. Have you met tomorrow's Theodora?

Of course! And most fortunately. But let me go back to the notion of a role model. I prefer the word example or inspiration. There's something of a command to conform in the term model. I'm frightened by this growing tendency, especially, it seems to me, among young women. The phenomenon of fashion is as old as the hills, but what's new are the catchphrases, the almost blind obedience to this new figure in society—the influencer. Oscar Wilde said: "Be yourself; everyone else is already taken." Every educational principle is based on helping the student or disciple first to know himself, to prefer himself to the sparkling personalities we dream of approaching in our lives, and then, in a second step, to find his own way by affirming the brilliance of his own personality. Nor should we try to be different at all costs. All the more so since we are all de facto different from each another—fortunately. Nevertheless, the standardization of attitudes, fashions, and even physical appearance frightens me—right down to the frequent and early use of cosmetic surgery. I'm afraid that's not the best breeding ground for artistic renewal, nor for offering the individual a horizon in which to find fulfillment. The more choices there are, the less the individual will be able to assert himself harmoniously. When I travel around the world, it saddens me that the streets of Shanghai now resemble those of Los Angeles, and that the way people dress, even the way they gesture—everyone with their faces glued to the screen of their cell phone—is the same in Johannesburg as it is in Helsinki. But, a role model does not have the same resonance as an example. The examples—the examples to follow, and who inspire—are the figures who don't try to influence us. They simply assert themselves in a way and in a mode of expression to bring a little charity, a little beauty back into this world. Some through art, others through struggle, and sometimes the two are reconciled. These are the women and men who do not hesitate to something greater than their own interests first—Johann Sebastian Bach in music, Dian Fossey in ecology, Mother Theresa in charity. Lastly, by reputation, LaDonna. The news sometimes highlights them when they sacrifice their lives to save others, when they take on the misfortunes of the world, the defense of the oppressed, of nature, of a thankless cause, without regard for their health, their life, their reputation.

12

HORSE WHISPERER

You moved to the West Coast to devote yourself to a new cause: protecting wild mustangs. What led you to become interested in a species that is so different from wolves? I can't think of this passion without recalling the famous story about Nietzsche, which is more than an anecdote, but an entire life in miniature: on Monday, January 3, 1889, unable to bear the sight of a horse being viciously beaten by its coachman, Nietzsche threw himself sobbing around the animal's neck. Taken back to his small room in Turin, he lay unconscious for hours. When he awoke, he introduced himself as both Dionysus and the Crucified One.

That's right, I've moved to the West Coast of the United States, but not on some a whim or new passion. As far as I'm concerned, I know exactly where my attraction to and love for horses comes from. They come from my childhood. My encounter with these fabulous animals in the Camargue is inextricably tied to memories of a very happy time. Not somewhat or just a little happy, but completely happy. It was they, long before

Alawa, long before the wolves, who first gave me that feeling of connection with the cosmos to which I am so attached, and my desire to live and run in the wide-open spaces, in my own way, without any constraints or barriers. In some way they were like a mirror into which I could project my future. They seemed to be endowed, oddly enough, with a supernatural gentleness, but also with something essentially fierce, pure and violent. That day, in the ponds of the Camargue, completely alone under the big sky, I tried to get close to them. For a few yards, I was able to approach them without them flinching—no doubt I was in the wind and they hadn't seen me. Then, all at once, they sensed my presence and disappeared like flamingos—in a great flight, haloed by foam.

Why didn't you ever ask your parents to enroll you in a riding school?

People have been asking me this question lately, especially since they know of my interest in the fate of the wild mustangs. The answer seemed to me so obvious it was already on my lips.

What I had loved about these horses of the Camargue, whose origins I later learned remain a mystery, even though their breed is thought to be one of the oldest in the world, was that they were tenaciously wild—by which I mean intimately connected to their habitat of which they are a part, along with birds and fighting bulls.

The drovers of the bull herds, who tame them, let them roam free when their owners are not riding them. There have been many attempts over the centuries to cross them with other horses to be used as mounts for war or hunting, but none of these ventures succeeded. The myth of White Mane* is not misplaced . . . And then how could I have reconciled my fascination with the essential freedom of these horses with the supervision and discipline demanded by the art of riding in a school? How could I have taken part in something that I dread so much for myself—being brought to heel?

Let's get back to the wild mustangs and your move to the West Coast.

When I learned of the fate in store for the American cousins of the horses of the Camargue—and at the time I thought it was just a rumor, one of those famous pieces of *fake news* that poisons our life—I decided to verify the information. To tell the truth, I would have preferred if it had turned out to be an urban legend. I don't know why but I feel like that I owe this species a debt—for having made me feel so light, euphoric, and blissfully happy when I saw them. So I decided to act, because these horses are now threatened with mass slaughter. Since 1971 a federal law enacted by Congress protects them from being destroyed by euthanasia or sterilization. But abandoned to their fate, these horses, an integral part of the winning of the West, whose image and silhouette shape the myth, were de facto abandoned by their former owners in favor of the automobile and released into the wild without any thought for how they would live. They then migrated in groups to the high plateaus of the Rocky Mountains

***Crin-blanc* (*White Mane*) is a French short film directed by Albert Lamorisse and released in 1953. The story is about a white horse that escapes its owners in the Camargue and bonds with a young boy.

and its vast spaces, where grass is short and rare, but with so much space in which to roam, they found enough to feed themselves. They thrived here, and although their numbers have dwindled from an estimated two million at the beginning of the century to about 50,000 today, the federal agency responsible for their management, the BLM*, estimates that there are 12,000 horses too many. The BLM estimates in the absence of natural predators that their population will double in the next five years if nothing is done to control their growth. They believe that the only thing that can regulate this growth is a weather disaster—one of those terrible droughts that are becoming increasingly common in the American West. While waiting for the heavens to assume responsibility for reducing their numbers, the government decided to trap them. In reality, the reason for this decision is that the high plateaus where they spend their lives have subsequently been invaded by cattle ranchers who practice intensive grazing on these thousands of square miles of government land. The mustangs, these farmers say, eat their cattle's grass and drink their water—water that is becoming increasingly scarce. Since they cannot be slaughtered, they must be driven out of the habitat that has become their natural environment since the advent of the automobile, airplane, and railroad. But how do you coerce animals that are so fast, so fierce, so wild, and on such vast tracts of land, most of which have no transportation routes? The helicopter provided an effective answer. For hours on end, the aircraft hover over the herds, skimming over them, driving the horses crazy and gradually driving them toward the paddock that awaits them. These terrorizing chases often last for hours.

*Bureau of Land Management

Hours in which the horses are relentlessly harassed. Many die during this infernal pursuit, some break their legs, and others fall into the ravines. An animal rights organization filmed one of these operations—surreptitiously, it goes without saying. The film was shown on prime-time television. Americans were horrified by the violence of the images: foals and pregnant mares falling over, dying of terror and exhaustion. They discovered how the stallions, driven mad in the corrals, attacked other stallions to protect their families. The public outcry and pressure was so great that these aerial roundups were banned . . . In time the public's attention shifted elsewhere and helicopters once again took off for the high plains of Nevada. Why does the weather matter? When it's at its worst—from cold to a heat wave—the pilots are guaranteed a high mortality rate among the herd during their mad dash. During a particularly hot summer three years ago in Owyhee Complex,* an aerial hazing killed seventeen of the Tuscarora herd's two hundred horses. During the following winter, in the Calico Mountains, five hundred horses didn't survive and forty mares aborted. As for the mustangs that did make it, they were locked up in tiny corrals. The stallions tear each other apart, the foals are trampled, and the horses bite each other.

What can you do to stop this slaughter and ill-treatment?

I'm creating a structure and thinking about viable, sustainable solutions. Today some of the horses captured like this can be adopted, but in order for them to find families to adopt them,

*In Elko and Humboldt Counties, Nevada.

they have to be broken in quickly. In most cases, breaking them in is brutal and quick. Others are destined for rodeos. Because horse slaughterhouses are banned in the United States, most are trucked to Mexico for slaughter. Such horrific, unacceptable mistreatment ends up being tolerated—like everything else. Or at least becomes something that people turn a blind eye to. And so, like the wolf, the mustang too will eventually disappear as a wild animal, in all its splendid beauty.

The film *Crin-blanc*—when I heard the rumors about these horses—determined me to act. As I watched it, I was reminded of a prophecy by Chief Seattle that I inscribed above my fireplace in my home in Salem: "He treats his mother, the earth, and his brother, the sky, as things to be bought, plundered, sold like sheep or bright beads. His appetite will devour the earth and leave behind only a desert."

You wrote this for the Korean edition of *Variations sauvages:**

> *The wolves forced me to become myself. Do they have something in common? Yes, like everything that matters on this earth: they are an absolute, the mirror of that other life that we know is the only quest to pursue. Music is wild, like wolves are civilized; both are the nobility of the world when it suddenly opens up to us and reveals its secrets. Music in all places is like the wolves: nothing can stop them. We can choose to suppress them, they'll come back. You can't kill freedom.*

**Wild Harmonies: A Life of Music of Music and Wolves*, trans. by Ellen Hinsey. Riverhead/Penguin, 2006.

Do you feel the same empathy and familiarity with horses as you do with wolves? I suppose training them or just domesticating them was a lot easier than with wolves?

Quite the opposite. A few years ago I was walking around in a ranch on the border of Yellowstone Park, and I discovered something about myself that I had never suspected: I'm afraid of horses. I'd been offered the chance to ride along a trail left by wildlife to personally evaluate the balance of species. I confessed that I'd never been on a horse before. They went to get an older mare whose sure-footedness, calm temperament, and gentle character were well known. I shuddered with fear as I hoisted myself into the saddle, a fear so obvious that the mare snorted slightly. Mat was amused by this paradox—that I wasn't afraid of wolves, but I was afraid of horses. I gritted my teeth the entire ride, my heart pounding, my muscles so tense that when I set foot on the ground on the way back, I could barely walk. But my day on horseback had a positive effect. When I came into contact with the mustangs, the fear, born of intimidation—you're always intimidated by what you admire—the fear that the horses inspired in me, turned out to be one of the elements that most strongly encouraged me to do something to protect them. It moved me so strongly that I temporarily moved away from South Salem and the Wolf Center, now fully operational and in the hands of competent scientists and managers, to California, closer to their natural habitat. It seemed to me that there was the same distance between wolves, carnivores and useful predators, and horses, herbivores and prey for humans, and sometimes for wolves, as there was between the sounds of nature and the works of classical music. I felt that by drawing attention to their plight after having drawn attention to that of the wolves, I was traversing the entire octave of my own score in the world.

And then there was also that unknown part of me that the horses taught me to tame: my fear. Fear, which I've always forbidden to dictate to me, so much so that it implies withdrawing into oneself or not trying anything unless you've first experienced the infinite number of safety nets that can be stretched around you, to the point of making them rigid, to the point of turning them into prison bars. Yet it would take a much stronger stimulus than fear for the world to change and improve. Beauty, love . . . and even risk . . . That's the risk I decided to take when I left for the West. "Go West young man, go West and grow up with the country." That was America's motto to its pioneers in 1865. I made it my motto when I moved to a ranch on the West Coast so I could collect mustangs and think about more concrete, more precise action, still under study. Of course, I've changed my motto a little: "Hélène, go West and grow up with nature. And with a vision of liberating liberty. What Rimbaud calls "the free freedom."

Horses, music, wolves, literature, the great outdoors . . . Is there a very personal activity that you indulge in privately, or that you reserve for just a few friends?

Actually there is one. But it's something I practice far away from other people, sometimes in the middle of the wolves, and often in the woods with my two hiking companions—my dogs Chico and Dude. More than an activity or discipline, it's a kind of secret, intimate ceremony: I dance. Not according to fixed rules, not tango or entrechats. More like improvisations. Like eruptions. In my mind I go over the score I'm working on and I start to dance. My body sketching the music gives me the magical feeling of projecting it into a fourth dimension, impregnating the air and my body with it. When I dance, I feel like I am fully participating in life. I focus all my attention on every pore of my skin, I stretch in the wind, I enchant my body, I free it from fatigue and rust. I loosen it up. Rarely does anyone take into account the muscular work and athletic effort required to study the piano. And I physically experience joy.

I dance when I'm happy or to release the sorrow or grief that sometimes besiege me. The first time I danced this way was when I was a child in the Camargue, in the reeds after the horses had soared off like flamingos. I had a sudden, irrepressible desire to twirl myself, arms outstretched to the sky, legs winged with drops of water that stole the sun's radiance. Later I discovered Nietzsche's words, which I've already quoted to you, and I had the feeling that he had written them not for his friend Franz Overbeck, but for me: "The animals with whom he was speaking, seeing his frustration, invited Zarathustra to abandon speech. He must learn to sing, as Socrates did at the time of his death. Ideally, the thinker must dance what he wants to say." I also discovered that there was nothing abnormal in this impulse or in the desire to dance in the midst of nature. In the Bible, which so fascinated me as a child, the Psalms proclaim God's invitation to a dance of prayer: "Praise the Lord! . . . Let them praise his name with dancing! Let them rejoice with tambourines and harps!"* Saint Augustine recognized the sacred nature

*Psalms 149:1 and 149:3.

of dance, and I found the exact definition of what I feel when I dance in the writings of Clement of Alexandria: it makes it possible ". . . to accompany the movement of our thought toward the intelligible essence. It is how we try to detach our body from the earth with our words, after having lifted our winged soul to the heavens with an ardent desire for perfection." In truth, dance has never lost its links with the sacred: it is "an act of faith and an act of love, it is a prayer, profane or sacred," as the great dancer Serge Lifar declared. Nietzsche again wrote: "I do not know what the spirit of a philosopher could wish to be more than a good dancer." And he made his Zarathustra a dancer, praising the prowess of Dionysus, who makes it possible for "The highest and the lowest energies of human nature, what is sweetest, most frivolous, and most terrible wells forth from one fount with immortal assurance." Nijinsky, the hero of the *Ballets Russes*,* embodied this praise of the vital instinct by defying all conventions in his inaugural dance of all modern dance, the scandalous *Rite of Spring* in 1913. And it is of this "I," other and strange, of its wild and free joy that belongs to me, that Arthur Rimbaud testifies when he says: "I have stretched ropes from steeple to steeple; garlands from window to window; golden chains from star to star, and I dance."

Like music, dance transmutes the heavy into the light. Thanks to them, the body is no longer an obstacle that has to be overcome in order to merge with the living; it becomes the life into which the music plunges in order to better reach the most high, the spirit, the invisible. Sometimes, when I'm dancing, I have the feeling that I'm composing, that I'm drawing out

*Ballet Company founded in Paris, France.

the contours and the splendor of the music. Then I feel that I myself am being danced by life, in a kind of cosmic hallelujah. "Dancing is the act of metamorphosis," wrote Paul Valéry. What kind of metamorphosis is this, if not the rush into words and the body to praise love?

I remember being dumbfounded by Pascale Ferran's film adaptation of D. H. Lawrence's *John Thomas and Lady Jane*—an earlier version of *Lady Chatterley's Lover*—with its scene of the heroine dancing naked in the rain, and the choreography of the two lovers in a warm summer shower, in the heart of the forest. This sequence exalts the celebration of sexual harmony and nature with unforgettable purity and sacredness. We're in the Garden of Eden, washed and cleansed of all pornographic filth. It's not only aesthetically perfect, it's extraordinarily intelligent; the scene offers a glimpse of the future and of hope, counterbalancing the memorable opening words from *Lady Chatterley's Lover,* which seem written for us, for today, for now: "Ours is essentially a tragic age, so we refuse to take it tragically. The cataclysm has happened, we are among the ruins, we start to build up new little habits, to have new little hopes. It is rather hard work: there is now no smooth road into the future: but we go round, or scramble over the obstacles. We've got to live, no matter how many skies have fallen."

You asked me when was the last time I danced like this, alone beneath the sky. It was in front of my dog, Dude. I had just returned from a trip in time to witness the death of my Chico, my noble protector, my knight in shining armor. There's always a sense of humility, almost shame, in expressing the terrible grief that grips anyone who loses a dog or cat. There is so much misery on in the world! So many dead people and children! And yet . . . I had grasped something of the magnitude of this grief when I discovered the pet cemetery in Paris that I told you about, and a few years earlier, when my grandfather's dog died. But when it's your own friend, your ever-faithful, ever-loving companion, when you remember the depth of his gaze, the way he questioned you when he saw your suitcases and the taxi coming to pick you up—"You're not going to leave me, are you?"—Remembering his joy when you put on your walking shoes—your dancing shoes—and set off with him to sniff the wind, and the deep, silent complicity that united your steps, when you hear his long exasperated sighs when he thought your rehearsals were too long, then this terrible pain overwhelms you. Chico, my shadow took on his shape. My hands, where he used to stick his nose for a caress, are still searching for him. The emptiness that followed him doesn't close. When I danced in front of him, he would lie down next to his inseparable companion, Dude, my beloved terrier. He'd look at me, his head cocked to one side or the other, before jumping up and capering around me. That night I had to get out of the house and find refuge. I took Dude in my arms and gently danced with him—just a few steps. I danced, so I would not begin howling like a wolf.

Yes, I dance, and I will never forget to dance. One composer always reminds me of this desire. It's Johann Sebastian Bach, particularly his partitas—and his suites—which at first listen seem like dances.

In truth, they require an incredible variety of techniques to express the very soul of the music as well as the soul of the instrument, like the exciting, excited *bariolage* that the opening prelude of Bach's *Partita in E major*—something ebullient and exuberant—gives us to hear. I listen to it. I practice it. I understand that this music must be, how shall I put it, "arranged" in a spacious way and at the same time played with the utmost urgency. I understand that I must add to it, like the pollen on the bee's legs after it has passed through the heart of the flower, all the spiritual charge that must always infuse Bach's music, with its characteristic waves of joy and euphoria, in other words, all the spiritual essence of the impulse to dance, captured in a sound. Why associate these Bach pieces (such as the Gigue from *Partita No. 3 in E major* or the Chaconne from *Partita No. 2 in D minor*) with dance? Because both offer the same key—joy. The cathedral joy that possesses them all. The joy of laughter. The divine joy of affirming eternity. Joy, as the only kingdom that music perpetuates.

I know that you like this observation by Claude Lévi-Strauss: "Both music and mythology are machines for suppressing time . . . it is as if in listening to music, and while we listen to it, we rise to a sort of immortality. . . . *Since music is the only language with the contradictory attributes of being intelligible and untranslatable, music is itself the supreme mystery of the sciences of man, the one over which they stumble and which holds the key to their progress." Do you have a secret, a musician's secret, a fairy's or a witch's secret—and not advice because you dislike giving it—that you would like to share with those who read you and who listen to you?*

It is entirely within the title of this book.

CODA

"When will we go beyond the mountains and the shores, to hail the birth of new labor, of new wisdom, the flight of tyrants and demons, to love—the first to love—Christmas on Earth?" Rimbaud writes. So when will we go? This year? Tomorrow? And why not, in the footsteps of Rimbaud, celebrate Rimbaud every minute, guided by the "kings of life, the three wise men: heart, soul and spirit?" Why not celebrate the spirit of Christmas, Christmas on earth, *hic et nunc,* here and now? So that tyrants may flee, so that the donkey and the ox may finally triumph over the demons that torment humanity. The fulfillment of the promise, the birth of a new work. That's what we all love about Christmas: this special time of expectation: for promises to be fulfilled at last—the most beautiful gift of all. This expectation makes the weeks of Advent a pause similar to the pauses offered by music, with the same moments of communion and grace, the same slice of heaven. "The song of the heavens, the march of the people," as Rimbaud once said. The song of the heavens and the march of the people together, at last in concert, so that we stop cursing life so much! My wish? That everyone in every moment, in every second of their life, allows themselves to be penetrated by this Christmas spirit just like music. Like at midnight. When the music soars into the sky at the same times as "the sun of the wolves" as the moon is called.

Appendix

A SHORT PORTABLE PHILOSOPHY

My morning rule of three

No one can help me if I don't help myself
If I only help myself, I'm nothing
There's no reason why I shouldn't act now.

Dignity

When you have doubt while working, never tell yourself that you are worthless or insignificant. We should feel our mediocrity only in front of spirit, beauty, and nature, never in front of people. In front of people, be aware of your strength.

Art

Why music? Why art in general? To escape from hell, to transform the chaos of this world into a piece of Eden.

Distance

Prefer music to the couplets of fashionable opinions. The only way to keep your distance is to rise above it.

Enemies

The more of a mess they make of their own life, the less of a mess they will make for you.

Your enemy? Those people who try to get you to despise the thing that supports you, your divine part.

Don't hate your enemies. They have one virtue—they force you to always get a hold of yourself, to persevere on your path, to refuse to let yourself become scattered. Your success and happiness come from triumphing over the traps and low blows they set against you in the hope of destroying you.

Choose yourself

Remain unique and singular. We can never find our place by copying the models or idols imposed upon us.

There's no reason to congratulate yourself for wanting to be Balzac, Mozart, or Leonardo da Vinci. We can only take pride in being ourselves.

Sharing

We can weep over the unhappiness and anxiety that plague the world. We can also console ourselves by sharing them.

Pain

Because we flee it, pain is also what builds us.

Freedom

There's power and there's might. Power is exercised over oneself—using one's talents. Might is exercised over others—which is why so many powerless people try to harm others to counter the expression of their power.

I am free as long as I retain my ability to choose between expressing power and expressing might. To choose between good and evil.

Nothing is easier than doing evil—it's within everyone's reach.

Silence

Be silent for at least one hour a day, until you hear the rustle of angel wings, and sometimes their laughter.

Pride

"I want to be everyone else!" a child told me.

"But then, you would lose your innocence."

Compliments

Believe only those compliments that are not meant to seduce.

Listen only to criticism that isn't meant to destroy.

Love

Don't confuse love for desire, nor desire for envy.

*Ame et amour.** I love the fact that these two words begin with the same letters. As if each enclosed the other.

I believe in love as long as it increases my freedom.

You have to love until love hurts.

True love is insolent. Stay that way, at all costs.

Principles

Whether it's at the price of shame or glory, live.

---

*Soul and love

Look only to the past for encouragement. For the future, avoid fear. In the present, strive for perfection.

You say everything is difficult? Aim for the impossible.

Confidence

Whatever happens, don't despair. It's our turn to live. Don't pass it by or leave it for others.

Faith

When in doubt, contemplate with all your senses. Then comes faith.

Death

I will take only my memories away with me. Live so that they are transfigured by beauty.

One day, we will be only a memory for others.

This will be our viaticum for eternity.

Vow

That what is mortal in me may be absorbed by life.

In the words of Marina Tsvetaeva: "To be a wolf in the deep forest of Eternity."